Advance Praise for
SPIRIT SON

Spirit Son transcends the topic of addiction, and the death of a loved one to an overdose, to illuminate a path to continuing your relationship with someone you've loved and lost for any reason. Because of her professional training as a psychotherapist, Robin Monson-Dupuis explores every modality to healing in order to help herself climb out of the darkness of her own grief. She bravely shares her personal journey of living with a child who is fighting an addiction, living in fear of losing them, and living with the searing pain of her loss. Readers who have tragically lost a loved one will identify with the suffocating questions Monson-Dupuis explores around "What if?" and the barrier this retrospection is to healing. Her ability to articulate the nameless emotions and experiences that inhabit "grief" and the opportunities to find significant and meaningful healing is a major step forward in understanding the science of grief. This is a must-read for anyone, literally anyone, who has lost someone they love, or is seeking to help someone through a loss, and wants to find their way to the reality of continuing a relationship with their loved one despite the physical/spiritual divide.

— *Tanya Anderson*
   Marketing Coordinator for Ethan's Run Against Addiction

Spirit Son reminds us that when a loved one is dying or gone, we are not in control of any miniscule thing beyond our own brave decisions to allow grief its stronghold. Monson-Dupuis flung the door wide, inviting a gutting of everything she holds dear, in order to arrive on the other side of something that threatened to swallow her whole. A naked and potent voice on the topic of sudden death to heroin overdose, Monson-Dupuis allows the gorgeous revelation that our sons and daughters are safe and potentially thriving in realms beyond their bandwidth on earth.

— *Leslie Rutkowski*
   Behavioral Health Educator, Writer, and Professional Advocate

As the loss of her son permeates every aspect of her life and threatens the very foundation on which it is built, Monson-Dupuis risks everything that is familiar and precious to embark on a soulful and courageous journey through the darkness of death to eternal connection. Feeling shattered and alone, she is compelled to find what will heal her brokenness and make sense of her world again. Monson-Dupuis shows us how the power of grief and the willingness to be vulnerable combine to transform even the most devastating loss into a new kind of spiritual strength, direction, and purpose. For anyone who has ever longed to feel connected with someone they love, anyone whose loss has been life-changing, and anyone who wants to find their way home...there is something healing in this book for you.

– Laura Riggle, PhD, Clinical Psychologist

Robin Monson-Dupuis is an extraordinary writer. Her informed and honest storytelling allows us to enter her life and understand her hurt as well as her healing. I carry her *Spirit Son* story in my heart.

– JoEllyn Schultz, LCSW

Robin Monson-Dupuis has shared her innermost, raw, honest feelings as she navigated telling her story of the life and death of her son, Ethan, and her journey to connect with him again. Eloquent in her writing, her pain was palpable as she searched for answers in making sense of a senseless act. What a blessing to look into the heart, soul, and mind of a woman who has endured so much and found God and Ethan again.

– Jeanne Hammer, RN

Spirit Son captures in print the journey of a grieving mother and traumatic death of her son from opioid addiction. With her gift of words, she melts together her personal reality and professional experience. She travels through deep grieving and self-blame along unexpected paths in healing.

– Becky Loesche, family friend

Robin Monson-Dupuis reminds us that it is not just the person with the addiction who is afflicted, but their families who go through so much pain and suffering and require equal attention in the healing process. Through her devastating loss, Monson-Dupuis poignantly describes her emotional response and difficult, but relentless, recovery experiences through the lens of a loving mother and family. She generously shares with the reader her use of many different sources to finally come to a spiritually healing and reconciliation with her son. The perseverance and strength (and vulnerability!) that she shows is truly inspirational.

— Lance Longo, MD, Psychiatrist, The Dewey Center - specializing in Addiction Medicine and working in the trenches of the opioid epidemic

As a woman walking a similar path, having lost my son to an opioid overdose just 45 days after Robin Monson-Dupuis lost Ethan, I understand the pain and anguish and doubt and blame she candidly reveals in *Spirit Son*. Her honest reflections of her journey through these past three years parallel mine in many aspects. Her willingness to ١are all and to explore so many alternative healing modalities to finally ١d her way to a new relationship with Ethan are awe-inspiring and ١ignant. She is indeed a Warrior and will light the path for many who experiencing similar losses that simply seem untenable when they r. A beautiful, inspiring book.

٦arney, MS
٤d, Health Science Specialist, Zablocki VA Medical Center

'٤ opens your soul to the relationship you could have with ٠ou lost physically to death. Robin Monson-Dupuis's words les of her and Ethan's relationship will have you thinking experiences. You may see that your dearly loved ones have ٠nicating with you. If you have ever yearned for connec-٢ lost loved ones, READ THIS BOOK!

٦re, Survivor of son Clay Davison's suicide
٠ Department Detective and Peer Coordinator

SPIRIT SON

A Mother's Journey to Reconnect with Her Son After His Death from Heroin Overdose

---

ROBIN MONSON-DUPUIS

Ten|16
PRESS

www.ten16press.com - Waukesha, WI

For information, please contact:

www.ten16press.com
Waukesha, WI

The author has made every effort to ensure that the information within this
book was accurate at the time of publication. The author does not assume
and hereby disclaims any liability to any party for any loss, damage, or
disruption caused by errors or omissions, whether such errors or omissions
result from accident, negligence, or any other cause.

This publication is meant as a source of valuable information for the reader,
however, it is not meant as a substitute for direct expert assistance. If such
level of assistance is required, the services of a competent professional
should be sought.

Dedication

I dedicate this book to my son
Ethan Jeffrey Monson-Dupuis

I am so grateful for the time on this earth that
God gave me to be your mother. I love you so very much
and I look forward to seeing you in heaven.

Also,
to all of the parents who have lost a child to addiction.
May you find some help here in grieving the loss of your
child and in connecting with their spirit.

CONTENTS

Part One

Part Two

Part Three

PART ONE

"Owning our own story and loving ourselves through the process is the bravest thing we will ever do."
– Brene Brown

Chapter 1:

SPIRIT

This is my story. My story of how I moved my body, my mind, and most importantly, my heart, through the sea of grief I found myself in when my son Ethan left this world. Those three pieces of myself were often floating, disconnected from one another after he died. I had no map for this journey of how to gather my pieces back together. I felt lost, unmoored, and shrouded with such enveloping grief that it caused me to lose myself and what I believed in, for a long, long, while. The loss of a child is one of the most emotionally devastating traumas a person can experience. There were times when I felt as though I was trying to move through a reality so foreign to me that it felt otherworldly.

After Ethan's death at age twenty-five from an accidental heroin overdose on December 27th, 2016, I felt I was flailing, sometimes sinking in a sea that was darker than black and bereft of any safe port. This sea of grief was not exactly hostile, but it was indifferent to me and my personal loss. Why wasn't the whole sea sensitive to the horror of the reality that my son was dead? How could it not wrap me with tenderness and comfort? Instead, tentacles of pain clutched at me unceasingly. This sea of grief dragged me down with sadness and sorrow. I struggled for a long time to find footing, some steady bottom from which to start wading out of this sea, to what shore I couldn't imagine—what would this world be like with my son gone?

My training as a psychotherapist was not adequate preparation for my lived experience of this trauma. How to breathe? How to think, how to cope? How to even *be*? I told myself that there must be a way out of this sea of grief—what was the protocol I followed with my own clients who came to me seeking healing after a loss? What was the way out of this pain? Frustrated that none of the interventions I knew of seemed to help me, I gave up trying to be my own therapist. I started by just trying to be with myself.

All my life I have been grateful for my other "Robin" self, the self that has accompanied me on every run and race I've done since I started running when I was fourteen. She is sometimes a shadow on the sunny pavement, sometimes a wise voice, sometimes simply a quiet companion. She cheers me on, props me up when I want to quit, and praises me for trying, not just for my outcome. She was silent at first after my son died, not knowing what to say. But she didn't leave me; she just kept walking this journey with me.

This story recounts how I got lost in strangling dark sorrow, and how I found my way out toward peace and joy. How my belief that God had abandoned me and my family grew into a renewal of my faith that God never left me. How I moved from judging myself as having failed my son to loving myself as a mother who did the best she could do. How I moved from grieving that I had lost my son forever to rejoicing that he still is in my life as my spirit son.

As I look back now, I see that everything has changed in my life. At first, I tried to live my life within the shocking reality that Ethan was dead. I thought that I only needed to understand and accept that my son had changed form—he was not really *gone*. I wasn't willing to stop having a relationship with Ethan just because he died. I wanted to learn what it meant to have a relationship with him as a spirit. A new relationship with him being a spirit, without his big, tall, physical body that I could see and hug, without his deep voice that I could listen and respond to in conversations he and I would have for hours. Yet, what I discovered in this journey was that I had to first submit to and embrace transformational change in my relationship with *myself* in order to have a relationship with Ethan as a spirit.

Over the long years of Ethan sinking into depression and addiction, I had drifted far from my centered self. As Ethan's addiction worsened, I had intensified my efforts to help, heal, and even save Ethan. Some will say that I over-helped, over-supported, over-protected Ethan. Perhaps. But it was all given to my son out of love. His father, Jeff, and I agonizingly debated all of our responses to Ethan for years in order to hit the mark of not too much support, not too much help, not too much protection, as he moved into adulthood with his addiction still tenaciously entrenched within him. How do parents get that balance right when you are afraid your child will die?

Once Ethan was gone, I felt that I had lost my purpose. What was I meant to do now? He is now safely with God and no longer needs my help, guidance, or protection. My journey toward shifting my purpose was arduous at a time when I didn't want anything more in my life to be hard or painful. But, in the painful fire we get refined. I now have a far better understanding of my purpose here on this Earth. I try every day to make sure that my actions are aligned with God's purpose for me. I feel that part of my destiny is to be open to doing Ethan's work that he is accomplishing through me. I hope my story can be a living account of God at work through my son and me. Ethan has taught me so much, and he is still teaching me.

I suffered other unexpected losses as I struggled on this grieving journey. I lost faith that my fierce motherly love could heal my child's illness, in the way that we mothers believe our love can heal our children's hurts. I lost my faith in the healing power of my professional knowledge and behavioral health training, so I stopped treating clients after he died. I lost my faith in my sheer willpower to achieve the results I wanted. I lost my faith in my husband as a partner with whom I should travel through grief together. I lost my faith in the humanity of my workplace when they did not accommodate me for the effects of my post-traumatic stress disorder on my job. Some friends dropped away, and I lost faith in believing that long-term friends would be there through thick and thin. Throughout all this—perhaps because of all this—I turned my face away from God. I was angry at God. I had believed that God with His mighty power could have worked a miracle that could have saved Ethan from his addiction and prevented his death. All grieving parents privately ask, "Why *my* child, God? Why did that other child live, but *mine* died?" In this journey I gradually came to accept that asking those questions was futile. Those were not the questions that helped me to heal. I regained my faith in God, others, and myself by asking how to *radically accept* all that I could not change, even as losses continued to rain down on me.

One morning in early January 2019, just after the second anniversary of Ethan's death, I woke up feeling inexplicably compelled to share my journey. I did not *want* to tell this story. I did not want to re-experience my anguish. It had mercifully softened a bit as two years had passed. When I started writing this story, that anguish was reignited. Passing through the fire of my experiences again, I was further refined. Whether it was Ethan's or God's voice telling me to share my story, I humbly hope it will be of some help to the thousands of parents who have lost a child to the Opioid Epidemic ravaging our country who are trying to find their way back to themselves, God, and a new relationship with their child. This compulsion felt as though it descended upon me out of nowhere as I sat on my couch, gazing out onto a bitterly cold and snowy landscape, holding my morning coffee. I started jotting down the milestones of my journey and six hours later, my coffee now cold, I had the shape of this story. I was surprised, and ultimately blessed, by what was revealed to me during the year it took to write my story.

How does a healing professional find healing herself? I slowly and painfully learned that I needed help from God and many others to find myself—my broken spirit—and then accept the healing. This process required more than healing my grief over the loss of my dear son. To develop a relationship with spirit-Ethan required me to learn to love myself unconditionally. Spirits exist in a place of pure love. They are filled with pure love—they *are* pure love. I needed to open myself up to giving myself unconditional love so that I could meet Ethan in that loving place. Despite my anger at God, He shepherded me through my slow, wrenching steps with wonderful grace and love just when I needed grace and His love the most. I also had the blessings of several dear friends, my soul sisters, who held my hand and propped me up many times. This journey has required so much of me that at times I wasn't sure I could continue. While I never felt suicidal, at night I took to repeating a childhood prayer I had been taught: "Now I lay me down to sleep, I pray the Lord my soul to keep. If I die before I wake, I pray the Lord my soul to take." I sometimes added, "God, I am not afraid to die. Take me as soon as you see fit. Like, I'm okay anytime, God." Some days I even desired it. Many days dying seemed easier than living through the upheaval of the very bedrock of my life that ensued after Ethan's death. His death was the beginning of the fire that raged through my life. I had to lose my former self, my former life, in order to heal.

In the beginning, my steps were focused on my mission to understand *why* and *how* Ethan's life could have ended so tragically. I wasn't intending to focus on myself. But as it evolved, my journey was being determined by something outside of my own plan and control. This journey has forced me to give up something I have always relied upon in leadership roles throughout my career and personal life: my ability to control, map out a plan and a goal, and execute it. As I gradually gave up relying on my own control, I chose—admittedly, sometimes only because I didn't know what else to do—to follow the rudder of God in my life. Through my prayer conversations with God, I have learned that God wasn't indifferent to me after Ethan died. God taught me that a good and meaningful life is not always a pleasant one. This Earthly part of our journey can be at times very painful. Some of us have more pain and sorrow than others.

This doesn't seem fair. But fairness is a humanly defined concept. I have given up trying to parse out what is fair for me to endure in my life and what is not. It is a mystery to me. I do see now, three years later, that God has manifested goodness, positive change, and healing from Ethan's death not only in my life but also many other people's lives. Through my visits with mediums and a shaman healer, I now believe that Ethan, my grandmother's spirit, and other spirits are guiding and leading me. Yet that healing came at a great cost to me. It took courage, humility, and all of the strength I had left within me after Ethan died. It has taken a long time for me to be able to perceive the goodness God put into my life. At first, I felt only the loss and heart-stopping pain.

In those first hours, days, and weeks, I was just trying to keep living—no, just keep breathing—following the shock of Ethan's death.

The utter finality of his death stopped my breath at many moments without warning when my mind allowed that reality to bulldoze through my fog of grief. I couldn't find solace anywhere. Yet, within hours after his death, Ethan already had a plan to help us begin to move beyond heartache to some peace. This was just like him. He was a sweet and caring person and unusually sensitive to others' pain. He had a message for his dad and me. He appeared within thirty-eight hours of his death to Radhe, a psychotherapist from my women's group. The four of us therapists had been meeting monthly for eight years to support each other in our personal growth goals. We started meeting the month before Ethan's illness began in September 2008. Ethan had never met Radhe, but he must have known how much of a sisterhood the four of us had developed over the years to have chosen her to be the recipient of his message.

Shortly after his death, our group met for our monthly meeting. I decided to attend, because I needed to soak up their loving support. Their three dear faces turned to me carefully, with deep seriousness. There was a pause, and then Radhe, our unofficial leader, turned to me and said, "Robin, Ethan has visited me."

I gasped and for a moment I felt confused—how could he have visited her? He was dead! I said, "Wait, what do you mean? He's gone; what are you talking about?"

Radhe explained that Ethan's spirit had appeared at the foot of her bed at 5:00 am on Dec 29th, 2016. She had woken up to a motion-detecting night light strangely turning on across her room. She got up, went to the bathroom, turned off the light, and got back into bed, wide awake. The light went back on again. Puzzled, she sat up to go turn it off again and immediately felt a spirit come to her consciousness. She said she had no doubt who this spirit was, even though she had never met Ethan. He appeared to her with bright blue flowers in his hands, a child's fire truck, and a teddy bear at his feet. He conveyed to her a loving message that she was to relay to his dad and me.

Ethan told her, "Tell my parents that they did not fail me. They should not blame themselves. I always felt their love. I love them so much, and I am so thankful for all of the help and support they gave me throughout the years…my drug use was on me and did not reflect anything my parents had done wrong. It was my doing. There was nothing *they* could have done to change it. Please tell them I am whole now and at peace. And tell my dad that I had a wonderful day recently with him when I was home."

Radhe went on to describe Ethan's spirit as "radiant." She said that while his spirit was communicating this message to her, she felt incredible peace and "utter rightness" about receiving this message. After Ethan left her, she said she became very emotional and began sobbing. She said it was not from grief but from "feeling touched with a tremendously open heart toward Ethan." She said that after she stopped crying, she immediately wrote down everything she had seen and heard, because she quickly began doubting that it had really happened. She handed me a copy of her notes.

I sat in a chair in her living room holding her notes, stunned, my heart pounding.

What exactly is a "spirit"? Prior to Ethan's death I had not ever been aware of a spirit being in my life, much less one trying to communicate with me. The only spirit I knew about was taught to me in my Lutheran Sunday School lessons. My unsophisticated understanding as a girl was that the Holy Spirit was the part of God that sort of hung out here on Earth to help guide us while God was up in Heaven doing the important things that God does. As a girl, I recall wondering, "Why shouldn't I go straight to the top and ask God directly for help?"

In the New Testament from the Bible, we are told that our spirit is that dimension of our humanness through which we can have a relationship with God. Our spirit is where we can relate to God while still in our physical bodies. So, our spirit is our soul, the immortal part of us, the part of us that will never die. Our soul is our truest essence of who we were created to be. When a soul leaves its physical body, we are assured that the essence remains. This essence never disappears but moves onto its next step in its soul's journey.

Other cultures honor and celebrate the souls of their loved ones, and in doing so, have a relationship with their loved ones' spirits. For example, the annual Bon Festival in Japan is a Japanese Buddhist celebration where spirits visit the homes of their families. Similarly, during the annual Dia de los Muertos (Day of the Dead) celebration in Mexico, families honor the spirits of their deceased family members and support them on their spiritual journey. This idea that we can help our loved ones as souls on their journey appeals to me now as a mother with a spirit son who is on that journey. This kind of support would depend upon having loving interactions with our loved one's spirit *after* their physical death. If that can happen, perhaps our deceased loved ones' spirits can help us on *our* spiritual journeys while we are still here on Earth! This is, after all, the very definition of a relationship: two, who interact back and forth to love and support one another.

If one's soul is the most real, important, and precious part of who they are, then shouldn't souls be able to connect with each other despite the barrier of a mere physical body? Even though I am a soul still housed inside a physical body, shouldn't I be able to relate to a soul no longer in their body? Why didn't Ethan communicate his message to me, his mother, who was desperate for his presence? Was there something wrong with me as the receiver of his message? Or perhaps it wasn't that something was wrong with me, but that I was not yet ready to receive his plea that I not blame myself.

I yearned to understand what I needed to do in order to have these types of interactions between myself and Ethan. Sitting in Radhe's living room holding her notes, I asked her to repeat Ethan's words out loud again. She did and then said that there was more to this message that confirmed for her that Ethan's spirit was truly determined to communicate with his dad and me. She told me that as the days wore on toward Ethan's funeral on January 3rd, 2017, she continued to doubt that Ethan's spirit had really visited her. So, after attending Ethan's funeral with Sally and Linda, the other two psychologists from our group, she told them the story of Ethan's appearance and her hesitation as to whether or not to share it with me. Radhe said she was worried that hearing Ethan's message could potentially make me feel worse in my grieving. I nodded, understanding her point, as this was exactly my initial reaction—I wished Ethan would have come to his dad and me with this message.

Linda chimed in and said, "I initially agreed with Radhe's hesitancy until I had a strange encounter with one of my clients the week after Ethan's death, and it convinced me that Radhe needed to give you Ethan's message." Linda described doing a therapy session with a long-term client in which she found herself impulsively telling her client about Radhe's encounter with Ethan's spirit. She said she felt uncomfortable, because it had nothing to do with her client's therapy goals, and she was always mindful to keep her private life separate from her work.

Linda told us, "You know that I'm typically very conservative about the use of self-disclosure with clients, but I couldn't stop myself from blurting out the story! Then I tried to redirect the session, but my client wouldn't let me."

Linda's client said, "Funny you are sharing this story with me, because a few months ago I had a very similar experience. A friend's adult son died of a heroin overdose, and soon after he died, his spirit appeared sitting next to me in the front seat of my car while I was doing errands. He told me that I must tell his parents that his death was not their fault, that he knew they had supported him in every way they could, and that he loved them very much, and he knew that they loved him very much. He emphasized that I must share this message with them because it would be so helpful to them in healing from their grief."

Radhe said, "We all think Linda was meant to hear her client's story as confirmation that it would be healing for you, Robin, to hear about Ethan's visit to me."

I nodded slowly as I tried to take this all in…but I just couldn't seem to absorb it. I went back to her house the next day and asked her to tell me Ethan's message and the whole story again. My husband also called Radhe and asked her to please tell him Ethan's message. We felt so hungry for Ethan's words, a piece of him.

I read Radhe's notes over and over again. It seemed that Ethan had made certain that Radhe would deliver his message to us by using the story of the other spirit's appearance. Did those two young men orchestrate this together in the spirit world? Is this what spirits do—generously help those of us still here on Earth? Was this really Ethan's spirit communicating with his dad and me? Could this be a port in my sea of grief?

After my second meeting with Radhe and her phone call with Jeff, she called me. She said that Ethan had appeared to her again during the night.

His spirit simply said these words to her: "Thank you."

Chapter 2

CHRISTMAS 2016

Dear Mom,

How is work going? School is going great! I've noticed you have been very tired, is it because of work? I've been really looking forward to Christmas! Have you? I'll bet you anything I'll be on December homework hall of fame! In Junior Great Books it's nice to have your own mom doing it! — I wonder what you got me for Christmas! Psss! Don't tell me! The snow is just beautiful, isn't it? It was nice to have the unexpected SNOW DAY!!! Are you excited? Your birthday is also coming up! Guess I'll just have to get you another gift. Not!!! My B-Day is also coming up. March, not to far away. I sure do have a nasty cold to fight off! Those really do stink! The house looks just beautiful with the numerous decorations! It's been nice writing this letter than being sick in bed!
Happy Holidays!!!

Write Back Soon!!!

Sincerely,

Ethan M.

Ethan's favorite time of year was Christmas. He loved everything about Christmas—the gathering of family, the same special foods I made every year, the sparkly decorations I put out around the house, the anticipation of opening his presents and watching others open the presents he had chosen for them. I recall the Christmas of 1999 when he was eight years old, he wrote me a letter and placed it in the "treasure box" that he and I used to place letters we wrote back and forth to each other that winter.

Ethan was attuned to others' moods and feelings, so I wasn't surprised that he had noticed that I was tired and needed more sleep. He loved receiving presents and would surreptitiously shake the wrapped packages under the tree with his name on them in the days leading up to Christmas with a detective's eye and ear—trying to guess what was inside. He also loved giving presents, and would walk up to one of us with his present for us in hand saying, "Try to guess what is inside!" He still did this during all the Christmases he came home while he attended the University of Wisconsin-La Crosse.

Ethan had remained in the city of La Crosse after graduating with a degree in Psychology and Criminal Justice in December of 2014, trying to launch himself into a functional and independent life as an adult while he was also working at recovering from his opiate addiction. He and his girlfriend, Ariana, were each spending Christmas of 2016 with their respective families, and then planned to meet back in La Crosse after the holiday. He and Ariana had been dating for about a year and a half since meeting at college. She is a warm, vibrant, funny young woman who can connect to anyone. She makes you feel as though you are the most special person to her when you are with her. During a visit to Greenfield that the two of them made to introduce Ariana to us, I was captivated by her, which Ethan noticed. He whispered in my ear, "I knew you would love her, Mom, isn't she wonderful?"

Ariana shared with us that she greatly respected Ethan's decision to be completely honest with her right from the beginning of their relationship about his history of addiction and depression. She described Ethan as the most "kind, loyal, and thoughtful" guy she had ever known. "He was playful and sweet, and I loved listening to him play guitar for me." She told us with a smile that, "Ethan intently listened to me and remembered even the smallest of details that I shared with him, unlike most guys I know. He had a way with everyone of shutting everything else out around him when he was listening to you." That similarity between them perhaps played a role in their compatibility.

By the time they had started dating, Ethan was no longer using heroin; he had decided to commit to taking methadone. Medication Assisted Treatment (MAT) is one critical part of treatment for opiate addiction, and methadone is one form of MAT. He was attending a methadone clinic daily in La Crosse. Ariana told us that she felt "so proud of Ethan that he was trying hard to beat his addiction." He was mostly clean during the nineteen months he was on methadone, other than a few slips using prescription opiates.

Before he lost his job working for an insurance agency in August, his income was too high to continue to qualify for State insurance. His insurance had been paying for his methadone. He decided to go off of methadone in September of 2016 rather than pay for it out of pocket, saying he felt ready to try recovery without it. We had paid cash for Ethan to have a longer titration off the methadone than the clinic would provide so as to ease his transition.

Ethan was excited to arrive at our home for Christmas on December 23rd after a grueling drive through a messy snowstorm. We were looking forward to seeing him, but we were also feeling some trepidation in those weeks leading up to his arrival for Christmas. We had suspected he had relapsed on heroin when he was home four weeks earlier at Thanksgiving. He had denied it, as was often his response in the past whenever we suspected he had relapsed. We didn't want to return to the days of disbelieving just about anything he said, so we decided we would welcome him home and pray that he would be clean.

Jeff and I were also struggling with feelings of anger at him for his harsh words toward us throughout the month of December. We had decided to set a boundary with him: we would no longer give him cash, since he had told us he started a full-time job on December 5th. However, he claimed that the Human Resources department of his new employer had made an error in his direct deposit paperwork, so he did not receive his first check. He told us he didn't have any food and needed cash right away so he wouldn't "starve." This paycheck problem didn't sound right to my husband, who as a retired police detective could almost always sniff out when Ethan was lying to us. So we said no, and Ethan vilified us in blazing text messages, saying, "You are the worst parents ever, how can you treat me this way, just letting me starve? Don't you love me? Don't you believe me when I say I will pay you back?"

On December 19th, Ethan called us and said his car was dead. We were once again in a maelstrom of conflicting emotions of wanting to generously help our son but resisting this normal parental yearning within us, knowing that giving him cash was potentially dangerous due to his heroin addiction. Since October, we had spoken very plainly with Ethan about his being at greater risk for a lethal relapse since he had stopped methadone. We had implored him several times to consider other forms of treatment during the ninety days that he had been without MAT. The recent angry, blaming texts from Ethan were not who he really was. It was a scary but familiar sign of how he had behaved during the years he was using. We decided to pay for a new battery for his car over the phone directly with the car repair shop so he could drive home for Christmas.

Despite my trepidation, I could hardly wait to see him. I will never forget the sweet look of anticipation on his face as he looked up from the couch when I walked in the door after work on the Friday night before Christmas. His grin was unguarded, open. His smile—his real smile—could make my heart just leap for joy. Could that genuine smile be a sign of him being well? I felt my usual scanning click into place as he rushed over to hug me—was he high? Ok? Depressed? I could smell smoke on him from the cigarettes that he had increasingly used as he was now off of methadone, but I didn't smell anything else. I looked into his eyes, and his pupils looked normal and clear. I didn't like this in me—my habit of examining my son—but it had become ingrained after more than eight years of trying to support him through depression, suicide attempts, hospitalizations, and substance abuse.

I was eager to hear about his new job. We talked as he and I made his favorite dinner together, tater tot casserole, pure comfort food! Cooking and baking were some of the things that Ethan and I enjoyed doing together. With him by my side, he teased me about the fact that I could not get away with sneaking a vegetable into the casserole, as I was known to do. I smiled at him sideways and said, "You know me so well! I was just thinking—hmmm, how could I distract you and add some peas while you are not looking?" His older sister Deva arrived to join us for dinner. As we sat together at our family table for a rare meal with just the four of us, I had a moment of deep thankfulness for this time with Ethan. He described his new job as a Credentialing Compliance Coordinator as "great," the people he worked with as "really nice," and then changed the subject to ask his sister about her new job as a psychotherapist. We were thankful and pleased to hear that his job was going well, as this was his fifth job in the two years since he had graduated. We didn't press him for more details. It was actually a relief to feel that we could perhaps take what he was saying at face value and let it go at that, as we had spent many years pressing him for details trying to get to the bottom of the truth.

As was typical when Ethan visited, he entreated us all to listen to whatever was his new favorite artist or his new favorite song. Music was his language, his sustenance; it was what fed him. He shared this love of music with his dad. Over the years, whenever he came home for a visit he would pull out the piano bench, plop down, and play something from memory. Or he would play a song on his phone and then finger it out quickly with his phenomenal ear. Sometimes he would pull out his guitar and start strumming and singing in his passionate voice. His voice would fill the room he was in, coming out strongly from his lifted face. Strangely, in the past six months he had stopped bringing his guitar home. It was a Washburn Cumberland acoustic guitar that his dad had given Ethan in high school when Ethan was teaching himself to play. We learned after he died that Ethan no longer brought it home because he had pawned it.

Tonight, he played "Everglow" by Coldplay on the stereo and talked enthusiastically about the melody and the lyrics. As I listened to some of the lyrics, I inexplicably felt a chill crawling across my back:

Life is short as the falling of snow...

When I'm cold, cold, cold...
I know you're with me wherever I go...

So if you love someone, you should let them know...

Oh, the light that you gave me will everglow.

I shook myself, stepped out of the room, and took several deep breaths, whispering, "Calm yourself, Robin; he is here, and he is safe."

His sister had to leave after dinner, but the three of us settled in to watch a Hallmark Christmas movie called *Angels in the Snow*. We all love movies. We especially share a love for sentimental— even cheesy—Christmas movies. I lit some candles and put Ethan's favorite snacks on the coffee table.

Suddenly, about halfway through the movie, he said to us abruptly, "Stop the movie, please. Dad, Mom, I have something to tell you. I have been thinking about what you said about my drinking so much at Thanksgiving, and I agree with you. I think I have a problem with drinking, and I want to work on that. Do you think I need to go to Detox?"

We sat there for a few seconds, stunned. It was the first time Ethan himself had initiated a conversation with us about his drug or alcohol abuse. We reached over, hugged him, and offered our support for whatever he wanted to do next. Jeff and I—mostly me—had made the mistake in the past of being far too involved in getting Ethan into treatment "one more time." At this point in his recovery journey, he needed to take complete control of those decisions. I flashed Heavenward a prayer from deep inside me: "Thank you God for this opening up in our son!" We were discussing what support he felt he might need when he was interrupted by his girlfriend texting him from her family's house in Minneapolis. He looked at her text and said, "Sorry to stop our conversation, Mom and Dad, but I am trying to be a better boyfriend to Ariana. I need to respond to her right now." As his fingers flew, texting her back, I felt a familiar welling up of hope within me that maybe he would be okay, that he would get healthy and it would stick. Maybe it was the fact that it was Christmas, but I felt myself allowing this hope to go beyond just a fleeting thought and lift my heart up in a way I hadn't allowed in a long time.

He finished responding to Ariana. We then talked about the work he was doing with his counselor in La Crosse, whom he had recently started seeing, and encouraged him to discuss higher levels of care with her or possibly other forms of MAT. We returned to the movie, which was an intriguing story about a family stranded in the mountains. They were rescued and spent a snowed-in weekend with a family struggling with grief and pain from the loss of their youngest child. The grieving family was deeply hurting, and in their hurt they were sniping at each other, disconnected, unkind, and miserable. The parents were not able to support each other in their grief and were on the verge of divorce. Over the course of the weekend, the rescued family was a healing balm to the host family; we watched the grieving family begin to soften, lay down their pain which was building a wall between them, and reach out to each other. At the end of the movie, it was revealed that the rescued family members were all spirits! They had, in fact, not survived being stranded in the mountains during the snowstorm, but had actually died. The family that knocked on the host family's cabin door was a spirit family! Ethan was amazed, as was I, by this ending, and we both agreed that we never saw it coming.

He said to me, "Those spirits seemed so real. I didn't know spirits could help people like that." I nodded, full of thought about the movie's message.

The next three days passed far too quickly. They were the best days we had spent with Ethan in a long time. We shared a meal with my sister Regina and her family, ice skated with Jeff's brother Chris and his family, went to church on Christmas Eve. We sang "Silent Night," holding up lit candles during the last verse. Deva gave him the most touching gift he received—a custom "19 months" sobriety medal on a ring for his key chain in honor of his ongoing fight for sobriety. His grandparents came Christmas morning and I made my traditional spinach quiche. He insisted, "Mom, don't *ever* change the menu for Christmas brunch; this is part of what Christmas morning is all about!" He loved anticipating family traditions;

I think they made him feel grounded. During his visit, he took his sister out for coffee, just the two of them, which I was happy to see, because their relationship had suffered during their college years due to his addiction and mental health issues.

Monday night, the last evening of his visit, we were sitting in the living room chatting with him about his plans for the week.

Ethan suddenly said, "My finances are a disaster. I don't know how I am going to pay my bills. I feel like a failure."

His dad said encouragingly, "You just started a new job, Ethan, way to go! Be patient with yourself. You will gradually get on your feet."

I added, "You said your delayed first paycheck should hit your account later this week, right?"

We got caught up in doing the math together, "…this many work hours since you started December 5th, multiplied by your rate of pay, gives you at least $1,300 after taxes. Ethan, based on what you are saying you need, you should be very close to making it! If you find yourself coming up really short, we can talk about us helping you."

He said in a monotonous voice, looking away, "I'm still going to be broke."

All of sudden, turning towards us, he said in a rush, "Can I move back home? I could get a job here! And I could get into treatment here, too!"

We sat there, listening, simply confused at first, and then dumb-founded by what he was asking.

Jeff looked at me, and in that split second, we knew we were in agreement.

I said, "No, honey, you can't move back here. Ethan, you know that we have set a boundary that you can't live here. Why would you want to leave your job that you said you like so much in La Crosse? And you told us you are seeing a counselor and have a sponsor in La Crosse, right? And Ariana is there, too; why in the world would you want to leave all of that?"

I recall him slightly turning his head away again, looking down, his face blank, and saying, "OK, yeah, I know, forget it."

He changed the subject, and shortly afterwards he and Jeff went out to a movie with Ethan's close friend from high school and his dad. We accepted his decision to change the subject, given our new mode of not pressing him in our interactions with him, and we let it go. Later that night after they left for the movie, I began to have thoughts that I wanted to share with him. Our conversation kept replaying in my mind. I felt so compelled to share my thoughts with him that I wrote him a letter. I placed it on his pillow for him to read when he got home after the movie.

Dear Ethan,

It's late, 11:30 pm, but I want you to know before I go to bed that I DON'T view you as a failure. I know and believe with my whole heart that you are a good person, that you are a man that can make a difference in this world...that you are someone who has something to give, and to BE to others that is important.

Your illness of addiction has covered some of that up, though...you have an illness, not bad character! PLEASE do what you need to do to cope with this illness. Please take good care of your SELF—your body, your mind, and your spirit that God gave you. You have such a great mind and a generous heart. I enjoy SO MUCH being around you when I see signs of YOU! That IS who you are.

Never lose track of who you are, Ethan. God made you whole and grand. You just need to keep on with the work of healing and overcoming your illness of addiction. YOU have to take the steps to be IN CONNECTION with people who are doing the same thing. You do NOT have to be alone or do it alone. Go and find those people and just spend as much time with them as you can. See what can happen that is good.

I love you so very much,
Mom

I am tormented by that conversation on the Monday night before his death the next day. I have rewound it over and over and over again in my mind, imagining various ways we could have responded differently to Ethan's questions, which frankly confused us at the time. I have chastised myself, telling myself that Ethan would still be alive if only I would have pressed him for more information or asked him to explain his requests. My husband does not share this torment. Jeff maintains that it was on Ethan to tell us the truth of what a desperate situation he was truly in. I learned later, when I explored the end of his life and talked to many people who knew him, that Ethan was basically living a double life since he had relapsed a few months before Christmas. His girlfriend was not even aware of this. I blamed myself for not putting on my "therapist hat" and treating the conversation more like I was his therapist, not just his mom. Should I have asked more questions? Should I have sifted through his puzzling requests as a means to possibly obtain more information and insight? Should I have looked for clues of a different reality than Ethan was telling us, coaxing out pieces of truth, perhaps even confronting him? Even now as I write this, despite so much work to quiet these questions, self-blame can still creep back into the edges of peace I try to maintain.

I had questioned Ethan with my "therapist hat" on many times over the years during his illness, always trying to stay ethically on the side of being just his mom. Why didn't I put on that hat during that conversation? I had vowed to stop doing that eighteen months earlier when he left Residential Treatment AMA (Against Medical Advice). It was overwhelming for me and was not healthy for my relationship with Ethan. It was also straining my marriage. So, in that last conversation, I stuck to my vow and didn't pursue Ethan. I accepted his decision to drop the conversation. If I had known it would be our last major conversation, would I have done it differently? My husband says that is an unfair and even cruel question to ask myself.

I now see that Ethan's death wasn't about me not asking the "right" questions. Right or wrong questions, he may have lived that day, but died the next. He may have lived another week, a month, a year, but died the next year. This was about *him*. Ethan stayed alive or died based on what he did with the resources and the support he had in front of him.

My letter to him that night was borne out of my love for him and respect for him as a responsible adult building what we thought was a fresh start for himself in La Crosse.

Chapter 3

ETHAN'S GIFT

Ethan planned to leave the next day, Tuesday, to return to La Crosse. That morning I was also to return to work after the Christmas holiday. When I knocked on his door and popped my head into his bedroom to say a quick goodbye, I was surprised to see him still in bed. He had planned to go out to breakfast with an old friend from high school, but he told me that those plans fell through.

I said to him, "Ok, how about you and I go to breakfast? I would love to take you out, Ethan, where would you like to go?" Often a meal would be a great way I could buy some time with Ethan, as he loved to eat good food. We agreed on the fact that breakfast was the best meal of the day.

He said, "No, Mom, thanks, but I'm going to go back to sleep, I'll call you later once I'm on the road."

I was a bit irritated with him because he had cancelled on our plans to go for a walk the day before and instead stayed in bed until two o'clock in the afternoon. He often cancelled plans during our visits depending on how he was doing. I understood this, but it still was irritating.

I tried again, coaxing him, "Come on, I won't see you again until your birthday, March 6th." He refused, grunting, "I'm tired." I turned, sighing, "Ok then honey, goodbye, drive safe." I shut his door probably harder than necessary and went downstairs to leave for work.

As I gathered up my purse, lunch, and workout bag for class after work, Ethan came downstairs in his boxers with hearts on them and he reached for me just as I was starting to walk out through the back door. The dear nearness of his sheer physical presence made my throat catch. He towered over me, all six foot three and a half inches and 250 pounds of my son.

He wrapped his arms around me and said, "Come on, Mom, let me give you a big hug. We'll go out in March for breakfast for my birthday. Don't be mad! I love you!"

One of Ethan's greatest gifts was his affectionate, loving nature. His gentle voice speaking in my ear, and his smiling at me the way he did when he was trying to win me over, melted my heart. His arms around me in a bear hug softened the pain I had felt the weeks before he came home for Christmas when he had texted so many terrible things to us. I dropped my bags and wrapped my arms around his broad shoulders, laying my head against his bare chest. I held my breath for some reason. I could hear his heart beating. For a long second I was transported back to when he was a baby and I held his body in my arms against my chest, breathing in his little boy baby smell from the top of his head. I breathed a deep inhale, and held him tighter as if I would never let him go.

The gift Ethan gave me of that last hug is so precious to me. I had no idea that it would be the last time I would hold my son alive.

Chapter 4
AN ANGEL
LIFTED ETHAN UP

That afternoon at 3:15 p.m. I was in the middle of a meeting. I had checked my phone prior to going into the meeting to see if Ethan had tried to call as he had said he would when he got on the road. He hadn't yet called, but that was not unusual. All of a sudden, I felt an enormous tug to call him that I couldn't ignore. It was an energy literally pulling me out of my chair, out of my meeting, right at that very moment. I stepped out in the hallway, and immediately called his number. I got his voice mail, and chattered into it as moms do when they are trying to connect with their child—no matter that the child is an adult—through the phone. "How is the drive going, Ethan? You must be a third of the way back if you left at two-ish as you had planned. We had such a nice Christmas with you, honey, it was so special, and we are so proud of you and your hard work with your new job and your therapist. I'm so glad you liked all of your presents! We will see you in March for your birthday! We will drive up there if you can't get away 'cuz of your job. I'm sorry I was grumpy toward you this morning, honey! I miss you already! Love you!"

Ethan left our home on December 27th, 2016 at about 1:00 p.m. with a $20 bill in his pocket he had stolen from his dad's wallet and a lie falling off his lips that he was leaving an hour early because he was meeting a friend for coffee before driving back to La Crosse. The next two hours we've deduced went something like this: he called his therapist in La Crosse at approximately 1:00 p.m. to set up an appointment for Friday, December 30th at 9:30 a.m. Then, he drove somewhere to meet a dealer. He bought heroin with the $20 he took from his dad's wallet. Then, he drove to a McDonald's in Brookfield, close to the freeway entrance onto I-94 going west to Madison. He parked facing south in the parking lot. He snorted the heroin he had bought. He opened an energy drink and placed it in the console next to him. He opened the sandwich I had made for him for the drive back and placed it on the seat next to him.

I believe he died at 3:15 p.m. when I felt that strangely intense need to reach out to him. I have fantasized that if only his phone ringer would have been on (he didn't like to keep it on for some reason), it might have jarred him to consciousness and he would have picked up. I would have known right away something was wrong because mothers can always tell, and I could have called 911. They would have rushed there and given him life-saving Narcan. He could be alive today to have another chance at recovery.

Instead, I try to take comfort in believing that an angel reached down her hand and helped Ethan, given his state of mind, to reach Heaven so he wouldn't get lost on his way.

I had heard somewhere once that seventy-five percent of heroin addicts who make it to age twenty-nine alive recover from their addiction. Every year he made it to another birthday alive, I would rejoice, fervently praying, "Hang in there, Ethan, just a few more to go, Ethan." Ethan was three years, two months, and ten days from that marker on December 27th. He would never have another chance at recovery while in his physical body.

I imagine the thoughts that might have been going through his mind as he planned and executed his last heroin use. "I shouldn't have stolen money from my dad...I'm so sorry...I should have told my parents what is really going on in my life; I don't have a job because I only attended two days and never was able to go back because I have been so sick with relapsing on bottles of codeine cough syrup, and painkillers I've gotten at Urgent Care by faking having bronchitis. I'm not really in any treatment because I've seen my counselor only twice in two and a half months because I keep cancelling appointments. I'm going to be evicted in five days for not paying my rent because I don't have any money, I should throw this heroin out the window, I should drive right to a meeting, or better yet, I should drive to the hospital I got opiate treatment at two years ago..."

I know that my wishful imagining of his thoughts reflects the faulty thinking that society in general has about persons with the illness of addiction. The belief that their behavior and choices are under their will power and control, rather than being hijacked by the deadly vice of addiction.

More likely, because this is what the demon of addiction does to the beautiful mind of a bright, loving, and beloved person, Ethan's thoughts were, "I'll use just one more time and then that's it. I just made an appointment for Friday with my counselor, and I also reached out to my sponsor—he and I will have lunch together on Saturday...See, it will be a fresh start for me...I'll be fine..."

According to the Centers for Disease Control, in 2016 there were 64,000 drug overdose deaths in the United States, two thirds of which were due to opioids. That was 91 deaths per day, as my dear friend, Je-Mae, described in her eulogy to Ethan at his funeral service January 3rd, 2017. There were 611 deaths in Wisconsin alone, and Ethan was one of them. This number was to increase to over 200 per day by 2019. Opioid related deaths now exceed deaths due to car crashes in our country.

I came home the evening of December 27th after work and an evening yoga class, showered, and checked in with Jeff to see if he had heard yet from Ethan. It was now after 8:30 p.m. Jeff had not heard from him either. This was highly unusual, as Ethan faithfully called us whenever he arrived back in La Crosse over the years he lived there. I texted his girlfriend, Ariana, who said she was just about to text me with the same question. She also had not heard from him, which worried her. Jeff contacted one of Ethan's roommates in La Crosse; he, too, had not seen Ethan all day. When Jeff ended that call, choking fear welled up in the back of my throat. I recall the exact time; it was 9:10 p.m. I put down the Cheez-Its I was munching on, and a sentient awareness flashed through my mind: "I will never be able to eat these again." Jeff, a retired police detective, went into his police officer persona. He got very calm and called the La Crosse Police Department to request they do a "Check on Welfare" at his apartment. We had requested this service for Ethan several years earlier, and they had been very helpful. This time they did not find him. By 10:30 p.m. the police began working on pinging his cell phone in an attempt to locate him.

At 11:30 p.m. a La Crosse police sergeant called my husband and said they had located Ethan's phone at an address in Brookfield, a nearby suburb in Waukesha County. Confused, we said, "But wait, that is only twenty minutes from our home, are you sure?" They carefully repeated the address. We grabbed our coats, putting them on as we got into the car and began racing, literally speeding, there. I had reached for the coat I had worn earlier in the day; it was too light for the freezing cold night, and I shook with chill as we drove. I don't think either of us thought to turn on the heater. We didn't speak. I quickly called Ariana and told her Ethan was located, and we were on our way to him. We bore down into the moment we were in—speeding somewhere to where Ethan's life was in danger.

We had done this four other times since Ethan was seventeen. Two overdoses and two suicide attempts, where we rushed in our car or on foot toward finding him. This had happened so many times that we had a physical and emotional response ingrained in us: everything else fell away; we had tunnel-vision focus on our son. I prayed out loud, "Please God, please God, be with Ethan, help him, hold him in your arms, keep him safe," over and over again.

I could feel us sliding into this crisis mode again as we exited the freeway in Brookfield. Jeff realized that this address was near a large mall. As we approached the address to what we thought would be on our left, I saw flashing red lights at a McDonald's on my right, and I said, "There—turn in there!" Swerving across three empty traffic lanes to turn right into the lot which was across from the mall, we pulled in at 11:51 p.m. Scanning the scene for any sign of Ethan, we saw his white Toyota Corolla parked and tried to veer toward it. We were blocked by a Brookfield police officer. We learned later that the La Crosse police sergeant had called Brookfield Police before calling us with Ethan's phone location. They did not want us arriving there first.

My mind quickly took in the huge red fire truck parked in a strange slant across the lot, a large white ambulance parked next to it, and two police squads surrounding my son's car, their lights flashing in, what seemed to me, an excessive manner. The whole scene seemed garish, like a scene in a TV show—bewildering to me. A police officer walked quickly up to us as I leapt out of the car. I remember being puzzled by how slowly my husband got out of the car. I burst out, saying to the police officer, "We are Ethan's parents, and that is his car. Is he alright?" The officer said Ethan was already in the ambulance and was going to be taken to the nearest hospital, about a ten minute drive from there. I begged the officer, "Can I please ride with him?" I had ridden with Ethan in an ambulance before while he was being rushed to a hospital after a very serious suicide attempt. I had felt then that by being near him I could somehow *will* him to be okay, to survive. I felt that desire now to be near him. The officer said, "No. You can follow the ambulance to the hospital and see him there." As we turned away to get back into our car, I noticed that there was broken glass on the driver's seat of Ethan's car. I said, "Jeff, look at all that glass!" He said, "They must have broken the window to get to Ethan." I was confused, my jaw clenching around questions that were starting to prick at my consciousness. I kept swallowing, swallowing, trying to keep them unspoken. Unspoken, so they wouldn't be true.

We pulled out of the parking lot after the ambulance and began following them west to Elmbrook Hospital. I turned to Jeff. "They are driving so slow, why aren't they going faster? And why aren't the sirens on? Why aren't they putting them on? Do you think Ethan is okay? I hope he is okay...Do you think Ethan is okay?" Jeff was quiet and kept saying, "I don't know, Robin."

It was later, much later, during that long night that he told me he knew as soon as he saw the face of the police officer walking toward us in the McDonald's parking lot that our son was dead.

We arrived at the emergency entrance, quickly parked, and jogged in through the doors. I asked to see Ethan, and we were met by a quiet male nurse saying words I couldn't comprehend, "Your son is in an exam room, but I'm sorry, ma'am, you will need to wait." Wait? Wait for what? What is going on with Ethan? I looked to Jeff, and he asked the nurse, "Wait, for how long?" We were assured that the ER physician would be there shortly. Shortly? We had rushed out of the house to find Ethan; we ended up here at a hospital and now were *waiting* to see him?

Standing there, I flashed back to a memory of the morning I gave birth to Ethan. It was a grueling birth, due to him being almost ten pounds and having a very large head. A business-like nurse took him from me soon after I held him on my chest and kissed him. Hours went by, and I kept asking Jeff, "*When* are they going to bring Ethan back to me?" Finally, though I could barely stand, I swung my legs over the edge of my hospital bed and began hobbling toward the door. "That's it. I'm going to get Ethan myself out of that nursery, dammit!" I remembered how it felt to say his name out loud, marveling that Ethan was indeed born, that he was healthy, and he was our beautiful son. I took strength from the miraculous reality of his birth and began walking toward the door of my room. I was going to go get him out of that damn nursery no matter what obstacle was in my way.

On that December night in 2016, I must have decided to channel that same fierce mother energy, because I found myself striding toward the closed exam room door, prepared to bust in to see my son. But this time, seemingly out of nowhere, a police officer stepped in front of me and blocked me. "You can't go in there, ma'am. Please sit down, and the doctor will be here shortly." Jeff took my arm and sat me down. I immediately stood back up. I shook with cold. Shock was slowly building as I felt pinned between two realities. Is Ethan okay? Is he not okay? I could not formulate any clearer words.

Just then the physician came around the corner and said softly, "I'm so sorry to have to tell you this, but your son is dead. The police are here because your son's death is classified as an Unattended Death Investigation at this time until the medical examiner arrives to examine the body. This is standard in this type of death. Please have a seat, and she should be here soon."

It was now 2:00 in the morning of Wednesday, December 28th. I called our daughter Deva to come to the hospital to say good-bye to her brother, but she did not answer. My husband then called the City of Wauwatosa Police, the nearby suburb where she and her husband lived, and a police officer went to their flat, rang their doorbell, and woke them up. They told Deva she must call her parents right away.

My husband called our close friends in our neighborhood to come to the hospital to support us. I didn't want him to do this because it seemed only necessary in the event of a disaster. I couldn't see this situation that way yet. They came right away.

How does a parent wait in this kind of surreal situation? What kind of cruelty is this? Waiting in a hospital lobby to be given permission to be with their deceased child who is locked in a room alone? My mind would not permit the possibility of Ethan being dead into my consciousness. I would not allow myself to think the words, as if I could alter reality by pushing them back. I waited, standing. I couldn't sit. I stood, an interminable hour, outside of that exam room, my forehead and right palm pressed against the door. I don't know if I was trying to melt through the door or straining to hear Ethan or willing him to get up and open the door. The police officer stood close by, unyielding, ensuring that I would not attempt to go in.

Finally, the medical examiner arrived, examined our son, and based on the history of his battle with heroin that my husband shared with her, released Ethan from the status of being an "Unattended Death" and allowed us into the room. Finally, able to go to Ethan, we saw him lying on a long narrow metal table. My first thought was, "That bed is so narrow, he will fall off!" I kept circling the table he was laid out on, looking at my son from every angle, frantically hoping to see a sign of life in him. I touched him, patted him tenderly, pressing my hands on him everywhere. His hands, his beautiful hands, were so cold. I tried to hold his hand in mine, but I couldn't bend his icy fingers. Oh, dear fingers, move! Curl around mine like you did as a boy! An orange stick that looked like a tongue depressor protruded from between his closed lips; it looked like it would be uncomfortable for him to have something stuck in his mouth. I wanted him to be comfortable. Looking at it, I suddenly felt in my mouth how as a kid it felt to have my mom stick a thermometer—the kind before digital thermometers—in my mouth when I had a fever, how I could barely tolerate it between my lips for the two minutes it took to record my temperature. I reached for the stick in Ethan's mouth, but I could not pry it away from between his lips.

His eyes were open. I stood very still, looking deeply down into them. His eyes did not move; they did not see me looking at him. He was not in those blue, blue eyes staring blankly upwards. I wanted to warm him, hold him, pick him up in my arms, climb onto that table and cover him with my body to make him warm, but I couldn't move his arm over to make enough room for me. I almost flung myself on top of him in my frantic desire to warm him. Jeff gently held me back. I moved again to his right side and smoothed his forehead, brushing his hair back. His hair blessedly still felt like him! His dark blond hair that he took such care with—it was him! I stopped moving around his body and stayed by his head. I bent down close to his head and smelled his hair; I breathed him in deeply like I did in the morning of this awful day when he hugged me before I left for work. My hands kept smoothing his hair over and over. It felt soft and not as cold as his skin.

A sharp sliver of awareness that Ethan's life was at its end pierced through me by the sight and sound of my daughter arriving into the exam room. She made a choking, gasping sound as she walked toward her brother. I had never heard a sound like that in my life. Her hand then pressed against her open mouth. She cried and cried as she kissed her brother on his forehead, bending over him for a long time. Her husband, also a police officer, stood looking down at Ethan, grief on his face. Looking at my daughter bending over her brother's body, it was as if I was not in the room, but floating somewhere high above this awful scene. I observed the pain on her face, contorting into something I had never seen on her before. Maybe this *was* really happening…she looked so grief-stricken!

How could this be? We had stood by Ethan in an ER hospital bed four times over the last eight years—and he stayed alive each time! He can't be dead; he comes back every time! Flashes of those memories rolled through me almost physically: Ethan intubated and on a breathing machine after he attempted suicide June 4th, 2009 (four days after graduating from high school); me, Jeff, Deva, her friend, and Ethan's girlfriend frantically searching for Ethan on the Root River Parkway. Jeff found him in the nick of time, unconscious, next to the river near our home. Two years later, we rushed to La Crosse and arrived at the ER just after his friend brought him there due to Ethan overdosing on his psychiatric meds; we kept a vigil as he slowly woke up. Then, another year after that, at the end of our weekend visit with him in La Crosse, he called us as we were driving out of town, incoherent, saying he had overdosed on his meds and alcohol. We drove through La Crosse frantically, trying to piece together his scrambled texts and phone calls as we searched for him for forty-five minutes and, thank God, found him next to the Mississippi River. We brought him to the ER, again praying for him to wake up. He *always* woke up. *Why wasn't he waking up now?*

Saving your child—literally saving your child from death—not just once, but multiple times, can give a parent the false sense that she has the power to keep her child alive. It did for me. Rescuing

Ethan several times from the potentially lethal harm he brought upon himself anchored in me a false sense that no matter what, we could keep him alive until he got healthy enough to keep himself alive, safe, and healthy, which is the ultimate foundational responsibility of every adult.

I learned later that it had been many hours that he hadn't moved or breathed during that long, cold winter night in the parking lot by the time I was able to touch him. He was found by the paramedics sitting upright in the driver's seat of his car after almost nine hours in twenty-degree temperatures. The physician who did the autopsy on his body kindly spent a half hour with me on the phone answering all of my questions about his death.

She told me, "Ethan died very quickly, probably within fifteen minutes of ingesting heroin. We estimate that was between approximately 3:00 and 4:00 p.m. We found an enzyme still in his blood that is only present when death occurs within about fifteen minutes."

I asked the question, "Was he in any pain?" knowing in my head this was a silly question because he had overdosed on an opiate, but the mother in me wanted reassurance from this kind doctor who was so gently telling me the facts of Ethan's death.

She softly replied, "He slipped quietly into unconsciousness and then stopped breathing. He did not suffer at all, my dear."

When someone slips into an overdose, their breathing slows, and may stop altogether. Narcan can very quickly cause breathing to resume, saving a life. In the spring of 2018, the Office of the Surgeon General issued its first national advisory in thirteen years—advising more people to carry naloxone, or its brand name Narcan, which can quickly reverse the lethal effects of an opiate overdose. This lifesaving measure only helps when one is not alone when overdosing and when Narcan is quickly accessible. Narcan could have saved the life of my son, who sat alone in the driver's seat of his car with a time frame of only fifteen minutes to be saved after snorting heroin on that cold afternoon. He was parked in a busy parking lot of one of the most visited restaurants on the planet, on the busiest retail corridor in Wisconsin during the post-Christmas retail rush. But no one intervened until almost nine hours later.

Who owns the body of your child after they die? I discovered that once your child dies, other entities and other persons take charge of that body, and you can't argue with them. In the ER exam room, there was finally the moment in which we were politely asked—"when we were ready"—to turn away from our son, our brother, on that table and walk away from him. I wondered briefly what would happen if I said, "No, I want to stay," or, "No, we will be bringing him home with us." The moment passed, and two men appeared carrying a long, narrow box, I assumed to hold Ethan. From a distance, we were allowed to watch Ethan being loaded into the morgue transport vehicle parked in the parking lot outside of the ER entrance and then be driven away. My legs quivering, I wanted to run after that truck and leap inside. Ethan—I don't want to have to leave you here alone! You are so cold! But I couldn't run; I was suddenly so tired, and my energy was waning. We turned away and walked toward the lobby where our friends were waiting for us. I looked into their faces and saw the terrible, heartbreaking expressions of pain and sympathy as we walked up to them. Seeing us as a family through their eyes—I knew then, deep inside of me, that this was a cataclysmic loss that would change our lives forever. I found myself almost unable to leave that desolate, eerily quiet, and ugly waiting room. I wanted to drop into a chair, just stay there, and not have to live through even the next moment.

But there was nothing left of Ethan there, so we slowly walked—legs, how are you even carrying me?—out to our car and began driving back home. It was 5:00 a.m. on Wednesday, December 28th. I instinctively took a deep breath—breath, how do you even keep breathing? How have you not stopped? I wished to simply stop breathing and not have to make this next phone call. I called Ariana on the drive home, closing my eyes as I heard her voice break when I said, "Honey, Ethan didn't"—she interrupted, saying, "I know. He's gone, isn't he? I haven't felt him for hours."

Chapter 5

NO PARENT SHOULD EVER HAVE TO DO THIS

The next seven days between his death and January 3rd, 2017, when Ethan's funeral took place, seemed to exist in a space wrenched and then suspended from the normal waxing and waning of day and night. I felt suspended in that black sea of grief, only able to make small movements that were absolutely required of me. Within three hours after returning home, unable to sleep, we were making phone calls that needed to be made to family and close friends, saying the words over and over again: "Ethan didn't make it." My heart felt stabbed with the fresh shock of the reality of those words each time I heard the intake of someone's breath or their cry through the phone. My dear friend Jenny, who had been with us during the dark night at the hospital, sat with us all morning in our living room helping me make sense of what to do next, and next, and next…tasks seemed to multiply by the hour.

I called Ethan's therapist in La Crosse when Ariana told us that Ethan had made an appointment to see his therapist on Friday morning. The therapist confirmed this, and I decided that I wanted to attend this appointment and talk to her. She agreed to meet with me. This was the impetus of our decision to make the trip to La Crosse as a family—Jeff and I along with Deva and her husband Jordan—with a trailer to get Ethan's things and meet with his therapist. I wanted to glean what I could from her so I could try to make sense of Ethan's death.

The forty-eight hours before our trip to La Crosse were filled with decisions that a parent should never have to make: planning a funeral service our son, making a decision regarding burial or cremation, picking out thank you notes and a service bulletin theme and photo, choosing songs, who will sing them. Who will play the music? Who will be the pallbearers? Do we want a closed casket? Or, an open casket with a "sleeve" to be slid over it later? An open casket with a sleeve would make the cremation "easier and it would be less expensive." My brain got stuck on the sleeve concept—what did that mean exactly? Having to choose what would hold his remains, who will eulogize at the service, what will they say? My sister Regina swooped in like an angel, attending all of the meetings at the funeral home with us, leading us through these strange and surreal discussions, helping us make many of those decisions. She marshalled her family of five children to bring us dinner the next night. I also kept turning to a dear friend, asking, "Should we do this, or this? How to make this decision? How to handle this request, made by this person?" My husband and I simply couldn't function as a team in making these decisions; we were too traumatized.

The only thing that I was fully able to handle was to write Ethan's obituary. Jeff and Deva and I agreed we wanted to be open and transparent as possible regarding Ethan's tenacious struggle with mental health and substance abuse issues during the last eight years of his life. We wanted to honor his fight, not hide it because of the stigma of drug addiction. We were united about this as a family. This was my comfortable space—words. With words I could make a tribute to my son's courageous battle against addiction. With words I could honor him, even though I couldn't touch him, comfort him, or help him any longer. Now, my story is the tool I

am using to honor my son and hopefully help those who are reading it and grieving their own loss. My idea then was to request in
his obituary that memorials be made out to "The Ethan Monson-
Dupuis Opiate Recovery Fund." In the hour that it took to write
the tribute to my son and create the idea of Ethan's Fund, the seed
of the work I would throw myself into after his funeral was born.

As the funeral date approached, dear friends and family arrived
from faraway states. Nearby friends came with food or hugs, sat
with us, and left. I often couldn't speak. One friend quietly helped
me with the emotional task of organizing photos of Ethan's life
to give to the funeral home. They were going to make a video of
Ethan's life to be played during the visitation prior to the funeral.
I hadn't looked at his childhood photo album in years, and it was
almost more than I could bear. I asked my husband his opinion
about which photos we should include. He said he didn't have any
opinion. I faulted him for that then. "How could you not have an
opinion?" I fumed to myself. I don't fault him for that now. He was
in some way more lost in his grief than I was at that time.

I don't remember if I ate, if I slept, if I made any sense when I
spoke. I do remember my son-in-law Jordan putting a plate of avocado toast with two fried eggs on top in front of me one morning.
I never had avocado toast before. I began crying at the sheer deli-
ciousness of it and the kindness of him making this for me without asking. I didn't even realize that I was hungry. This disconnect
within me reminded me that after I gave birth to Ethan, my body
didn't resume working in many of its functions for days because of
the physical trauma of birthing an almost ten pound baby. My body
stopped working now, too, at the time of his death.

This was the most exquisite gift people gave us in those first terrible hours, days, and weeks: not asking what we needed, just showing up, being present, maybe bringing something, doing something.

Not asking many questions about what we needed, because they somehow knew it was such a burden for us to answer those questions. We did not know what we needed after the death of our son, we could not know this, no parent should have to know this! I had only one need that I could verbalize—to feel my son alive—and that was something no one could give to me.

We returned home from our trip to La Crosse on the last day of 2016 with a trailer packed full of the physical remains of our son's life. Once we started dismantling his room, it was upsetting, especially for Deva, to see the dirty state of Ethan's room and belongings. This was so unlike him, as he was always a very neat and tidy person. His laptop and guitar were gone. There were no signs left in his room of his love for music. His room revealed to us a person whose life was in disarray just below the surface.

Immediately, our house swelled fuller with my family, Jeff's family, Deva's wonderful girlfriends who were like sisters to her, my son's sweet girlfriend, her mother Tanya and her little sister (neither of whom we had ever met), and my best friend JeMae and her family from Minnesota. It was New Year's Eve—how dare there be a holiday to celebrate! My sister-in-law Veronica arrived with food and no expectations for any celebration, she just provided her love and sustenance. I sat with the all of these dear people and heard their kind words and normal chattering. I thought I was going to scream, the scream that had been buried inside of me since I had seen my son driven to the morgue. I swallowed my scream and went upstairs to my bed and buried myself under quilts. JeMae noticed my leaving and quietly followed me upstairs and climbed into bed with me with her phone. Before I knew it, we were on the funeral home website looking at the flower arrangements that people had ordered for Ethan's funeral which was to be held in just three days.

The arrangements were beautiful, with a predominance of blue flowers; I thought it might be because everyone who knew Ethan knew he had the bluest eyes! What soothed my heart even more were the names of the floral arrangements. Names such as "Love's Journey," "Strength and Solace," and "Divine Peace." These words were like a balm to my motherly heart. The funeral home knew what they were doing, naming flowers with such hopeful words, like "Guiding Light" and "Sapphire Skies." I kept repeating them out loud, delighted for some reason at the sounds of the beautiful words. My friend shushed me like a mother would when I started crying for the twelfth time that day, and I slowly relaxed and dozed, the sounds of those lovely words washing over my wounded spirit.

The service honoring our son's life was delayed due to the New Year's Day holiday falling on a Sunday, therefore many people had Monday, January 2nd off as a holiday, as did our church's staff. So, we decided to wait until Tuesday, January 3rd. Initially, that seemed so far away from our son's death a full week before, but time moves as it does with no regard to events either joyous or tragic, and that day came so fast that I woke up that morning panicked. Had we planned the service adequately? Had I planned the dinner after the funeral at the restaurant that Ethan loved with enough food? Had I invited the right family and friends to the dinner? I had forgotten the fact that I needed an appropriate outfit to wear, so totally unlike me. Did I have a black dress? How was I going to feed all of our houseguests the morning before we left for the funeral?

I wanted someone to take over all of these details. I am a meticulous planner and organizer, but these responsibilities flummoxed me. As it turned out, I didn't order enough food for the dinner. We inadvertently neglected to invite certain key people to the dinner. Thankfully, we had a friend generously give us a breakfast casserole that seemed to multiply like Christ's loaves and fish did to feed the three thousand. It fed our thirteen that morning.

I woke very early from a fitful sleep full of disturbing dreams and went to Barefoot Haven, the yoga studio where I teach, accompanied by my nephew's girlfriend, Gina, also a yoga teacher. Her gift to me that terrible morning was guiding me through a yoga practice that would help to ready me—as much as a parent can be ready to attend their child's funeral—for what would be one of the hardest things I would ever have to do in my life. As I moved to the prompting of her soothing voice and adjusting hands, time seemed to slow, and stop still. She guided me to Pigeon Pose, a pose of deep submission and restfulness. I wanted to stay in this pose forever and not leave the safety of the calm, softly lit studio. To not face what felt like a gauntlet before me. My brother Rolf had predicted there would likely be a long receiving line prior to the funeral.

If you have ever been in Pigeon Pose for long, your body decides for you when it has had enough, and you simply have to get up. Move your hip and unwind your leg. One's body can't stay still forever in Pigeon Pose out of sheer will. It has a will of its own and that is to free itself of discomfort. I moved out of Pigeon Pose and into the day of honoring my son's life.

Back at home, I was staring, unseeing, out the window and drinking a cup of coffee, almost irritated with myself for enjoying the warm drink. My sister Regina called, interrupting my unkind thought, saying that she may be late to the funeral, as she wanted to make sure that she obtained Ethan's thumbprint to have cast as a pendant for me. I told her, "Regina, don't stress, it's too much, just do it tomorrow, it's okay." She was silent and then carefully said, "I *have* to do it this morning, Robin, Ethan won't be here tomorrow." I was confused for a moment. Understanding suddenly hit me, and trying to breathe, I said, "I…didn't realize…alright, of course."

I tend to be late. We were only *slightly* late that day to the church—because of me—but none of us thought it was a problem until we saw the line of people already outside of our church waiting for us. My mother and stepdad were the first to arrive and were waiting to greet us with hugs. Jeff and I, and Deva and Jordan, quickly assembled ourselves in a semicircle to one side of Ethan's open casket at the far end of the atrium. We had decided that it was important for our friends and family to see Ethan, to touch his body. My heart stopped as I stood and gazed down upon my son—looking oh so different from that night in the ER a week ago. He looked peaceful, the orange stick removed from his lips, his eyes now softly closed; such long eyelashes he had! I had forgotten that about him. He was dressed for the first time in the handsome blue sweater that his girlfriend Ariana had given him for Christmas. How did this miracle occur that he looked so well? I had grown accustomed to my child's body no longer needing my attention as he grew up into a large and strong man, but I still marveled at the transformation before my eyes—who had swooped over him and cared for him so well in the seven days since I had seen him? I wanted to bend down and kiss him, but he was laid so deeply into the white satiny bed of the casket liner that I couldn't reach him, so I kissed my fingertips instead and pressed them upon his cheek. I wanted to have paused there longer, but someone called my name, and I had to turn away from my son.

The flower arrangements were already thoughtfully displayed throughout the atrium and around Ethan's casket. Ah, those confections of flower and leaf, ribbons and crosses, this is what those beautiful words described on the funeral home's website! My eyes rested upon each vase of flowers, one after another, throughout the atrium of our church. Someone brought a stool for me sit on and for my daughter, too. I thought that was odd. Little did I know how much she and I would rest for precious seconds on those stools as the hours wore on. Waves upon waves of people came, stretching outside the church doors even in the cold: from my work, from the Greenfield Police Department where Jeff had retired from three years earlier, other police departments in the area, Ethan's high school friends, our church friends, and people I didn't even know. It went on for what seemed like hours and hours, because it was. I became overwhelmed by the sheer love and respect shown to our family. My brother became concerned for me, circling behind me and checking in with me. My sweet colleague, Carrie, came through the line twice, saying she had wanted to make sure I was okay. My brother finally whispered in my ear that he was going to cut off the line soon, as the service was already delayed. He told me Regina had finally arrived. Someone in the line hugged me who had been drinking; I smelled alcohol on her as she embraced me. I didn't care. I wished I had something, too, that could anesthetize me from the responsibility of responding to all of the people.

Turning away slightly in the line, I closed my eyes and whispered. Are you here, Ethan? Do you see all of these people who love you? I told you that you weren't a failure! You are *loved*. See all of the people? Do you see all of them? Please believe this truth about yourself!

The service began. We were guided to the front row of the church. Where are you, Ethan? You are there, in the front of the church now, the lid of the casket closed on your face. I'm sorry, this is an unforgivable indignity, you would have wanted to watch this. The music that Ethan loved filled the church, the video rolled of his life up on the big screens, the pastor spoke words which I cannot remember. I kept swallowing a scream that I felt at the back of my throat. I felt my legs shaking. Jeff clasped my right hand and pressed our hands against my thigh. His stilling me reminded me of my dad trying to quell my bouncing legs as a child in church. I could feel the trembling of Jeff's hand as his held mine tightly.

The service ended. Ethan was starting to be carried down the aisle by the grim-faced pallbearers. He was in the pretend casket we had ordered, holding the box that would be slid into the cremato-rium. Is that where you are going now? He was even with my row. He moved past our row. I lunged out of the pew past my husband who was on my right. I stumbled toward my son going down the aisle. The scream that I had bottled up inside of me since I saw my son in the ER seven days earlier finally let loose, and I cried out, "Ethan, Ethan!" Of its own volition, my body flung itself toward the casket; I steadied myself from falling as my hands grappled to find a place to reach Ethan. The pallbearers paused, shifting uncertainly—are there instructions for this type of occurrence?—but they stood still, respecting my need to pause their progress down the aisle for a moment. Then as one, they started moving again down the aisle. I walked next to my son in that box, weeping, patting the wood as if it was Ethan I was touching.

Within three days of Ethan's funeral, my sisters, my best friend and her husband and daughter, Ethan's girlfriend and her mother, my nephew Joel who is like a son to me, and his girlfriend Gina had all left and returned to their lives. Most of them had stayed with us in our home, keeping the air full of conversation and love. I took several weeks of a leave of absence from my demanding man-agement job in corporate health care. My daughter had to return to work. I worried for her, having to go back so soon to her psychotherapist job which demanded so much giving of herself to her clients. My brother thankfully stayed. On January 5th, my birthday, we hiked for a long time in the cold, snowy woods together. During a long silence, he asked me, "What are you thinking about, sister?" I said, "I am trying not to think. I'm just trying to breathe and listen to the snow crunch as I walk. That's all I can do." He nodded. The next day Rolf, too, flew back home.

On the sixth day after Ethan's funeral, my husband refused to cancel his travel plans and left for a week-long conference in Texas. I was left completely and utterly alone. I was angry at him for leaving, even though he explained that he needed to get out of the house. The way we each we grieving was so different; it was hard to find a place to meet each other emotionally. Our house, which had been filled with caring and supportive people and their energy for ten days, was now empty. The mid-January days were gray and icy. The house was cold, and I couldn't seem to get warm. I woke up each morning stunned to see the light outside returning again after a dark night.

In those early lonely days, I had two activities that held my interest: writing thank you notes and caring for the beautiful, dying flowers. These activities gave me comfort. The house was filled with at least twenty vases of flowers, plants, and elaborate floral arrangements from Ethan's funeral. In our church, these arrangements seemed to be a normal size, but in our house they were enormous, greenhouse-sized. I was so grateful for those living plants and fragrant flowers, so lush in their colors of blues, creams, purples, and whites. Each day, I moved slowly through the rooms. I changed the water in the vases, meticulously cut the ends of the stems to encourage the flowers to stay alive, pulled out individual stems as they wilted, and turned the green plants a quarter turn towards the light. My fingers smoothed the curling satin ribbons that said, "Beloved Son," "Dear Brother," and "Rest in Peace." I fussed over the flowers anxiously, entreating them to perk up, noticing that despite my great care, they were gradually dying. I became tearful when I finally had to throw away the dead flowers. I didn't want them to die. When the last arrangement of periwinkle blue, hopeful yellow, and white flowers finally wilted, it was still so surprisingly tender in its hues that I couldn't bear to throw it away. I gently picked off all of the dried blossoms and put them into a pink glass candy dish with a lid and placed it in my china cabinet.

In that week, in between caring for the flowers, I wrote thank you notes. I wrote over two hundred notes, slowing down my pace as I got to the end of my list to make it last longer. Each note allowed me to write my dear son's name—Ethan, Ethan, Ethan—again and again. I felt closer to him when I wrote his name. I said it out loud sometimes as I wrote it. I thanked the giver for their donation to the fund we established in his name, the "Ethan Monson-Dupuis Opiate Recovery Fund." Every time I wrote the fund's name, I felt that something good was growing, amidst the softly drooping, dying flowers. I felt I was now moving a bit *through* the black sea of grief.

Each morning, I settled into my chair at the head of our dining room table, with stacks of beautiful thank you notes with Ethan's picture on them on one side of me, my list on the other, stamps and return address labels in front of me. I would sit there for hours, feeling grounded in this task during a time when I did not feel it was safe to be any place, with mostly any people. As I wrote, I burned a candle the funeral home had given us. It is a heavy glass cube on a square mahogany base, with the four glass double panels each holding a different image between the panels. One panel is the obituary photo of Ethan smiling, another is of a bird soaring in a blue sky, another is the Serenity prayer, another is the words

"Strength, Hope, Love" intertwined together. The candle flickering inside made his face appear to have fluidity, the way a face does when it is alive, exhibiting many minute shifts in its countenance as it blinks, and breathes, and reacts to the world around it. I would stare at Ethan's face illuminated by the candlelight and cry out to him, "Ethan, where are you? Ethan, I am so sorry...what could I have done to help you? What could I have done?"

At the end of my week alone, the funeral home called and said Ethan's cremains were ready for pickup. I listened to that voicemail several times, trying to take in what I was hearing. The first time I listened to it, I didn't understand what the word "cremains" meant. I didn't want to go out of the house, because I had not showered or changed my clothes for a week. I put on the biggest coat I could find and drove to the funeral home, which was not far from our house. I sat in my car, took a deep shuddering breath, and then walked into the building. I was met by a business-like man who asked me to sign a form and told me he would be right back. My heart started to beat hard, really hard, as I stood at the table with the signed document in front of me. He reappeared with a box, the very box my sister had helped us choose for Ethan two weeks ago. He handed it to me and said, "Here you go." I paused, expecting there to be something more—a hug from him or a kind word. I lifted the box up and almost staggered. It was shockingly heavy. I shifted my foot placement and lifted again. The man asked me, as if I were at the grocery store with a cart full of groceries, "Do you need help out to your car?" I screamed in my head, "Help? Help? Yes, I need help in the most elemental way, help me to understand this—where is my son? He can't be contained in a box six inches high and seven and a half inches wide!" Out loud, I said, "No, thank you."

I carried Ethan out to my car, holding the box tightly to my chest, snow flurries blowing and stinging my face and hands. I dared not put my mittens on for fear that I might drop the box—drop Ethan. I had a sudden memory of the day we brought Ethan home from the hospital after he was born. It was a day just like this—cold, with snow flurries blowing into our faces. I remember being so concerned to protect his vulnerable body from the blowing snow as we exited the hospital, Jeff pushing me in a wheelchair with Ethan on my lap, his two-year-old big sister, Deva, importantly holding onto his little hand and refusing to let go. I felt that same way now, as I curled my body against the wind swirling around the glossy piano wood box that held my son.

Chapter 6
FRACTURED FAMILY

Healing from the death of a loved one is made more difficult if the death is sudden and if the death is from an illness where society judges it from one's own hand, such as addiction or suicide. The family of a child who dies suddenly of a drug overdose is a circle of stunned and traumatized people, who, though they love each other, may be completely unable to support one another in the aftermath of such a shocking loss. Each one moves through their days, just trying to keep their head above the water line of sucking grief to prevent it from pouring down their throat and drowning them. They move in a small orbit of survival, often unable to comfort each other. When they may have the strength to reach out to each other, it may not be when the comfort was needed or what was needed.

The family of a terminally ill person may have time to gather around their loved one prior to the death, hug and kiss their loved one, share stories, offer forgiveness to each other, maybe even laugh together. There is no such scene for someone who dies of a drug overdose. Unlike a person with a terminal illness who may have accepted their impending death and perhaps even "glimpsed Heaven" as their death became imminent, the person with the illness of addiction who dies from an accidental overdose often dies alone, with no awareness that they are at the end of their life on Earth. There is no opportunity for families and their loved ones who overdosed to say things that they may have needed to say to each other. Such as words of making amends, of forgiveness, of love, of honoring their loved ones for their courage in the face of the addiction, or of instructions given regarding what they were leaving behind. No last hug, no clasping of fingers, no cradling their loved ones' cheeks in their cupped hands.

I was often beside myself with remorse and regret that we didn't have those last moments with Ethan. Our relationship with Ethan as parents had been marked for so long with angst, fear, unrelenting worry, frustration, and even anger toward him regarding his behavior and his decisions to not maintain consistent recovery practices. There was no last opportunity for repairs in our relationship with Ethan. One moment he was simply driving back to La Crosse, and the next moment he was dead.

In the years prior to Ethan's death, Jeff and I had frequently operated in crisis mode, stressed as we constantly negotiated the decisions we had to make as our son went from a seventeen-year-old high school senior on top of the world, to a depressed, anxious, even suicidal young adult starting to self-medicate, and then to an adult man with a seriously life-threatening opiate addiction. We also both had demanding jobs. We actually managed these times of crisis incredibly well, almost always agreeing on how to handle our responses to Ethan regarding how to best support him, how to set boundaries, how to not enable him, and how to never turn our backs on him, ever. Our marriage, however, inexorably received less and less of our nurturing and attention as we were emotionally and physically tending to our son.

Often preceding the death of someone with the illness of addiction are months and even years of the symptoms of their illness slowly wearing away or viciously splintering the family bonds. Lying, stealing, inappropriate or embarrassing actions or words at family or public events, or not showing up at all—these are some of the behaviors families of a person with addiction have to cope with. Fear clamped our hearts like a vise when we saw Ethan behaving in these ways, because we knew he was not following his recovery plan. Ethan stole money from us and his friends. He attended family functions and celebrations under the influence of drugs. He didn't keep commitments he made to us. He would be a no-show for phone calls he planned with us, as we tried to be available to him in our long-distance relationship. His sister got married six months before he died, and she struggled with frustration and irritation with his lack of follow-through with the responsibilities of his role in her wedding as an usher.

As addiction worsens, self-absorption crowds out the addicted person's ability to be in healthy relationships with the people that he or she loves. These are normal symptoms of the illness of addiction, yet these behaviors can cause incredibly painful schisms between the addicted person and their family. Either families sharply fracture and break apart, or they are slowly worn down—my husband likened it to Chinese water torture—by the stress of trying to love someone with the illness of addiction. By the time Ethan died, so many of our family's physical and emotional resources had been depleted trying to help our son during the eight years of his illness. Too many of our family's conversations centered around how Ethan was doing. Our daughter often felt overlooked. When I told her that I felt so sad about that, she said, "It is nothing you could have changed, Mom. We all suffered each in our own way."

The price of sacrificing attention to our marriage for all of these years was actually most evident when Ethan seemed to be doing better and we became more aware of our disconnection and estrangement. I, especially, threw myself into helping Ethan. I tried to pour into his heart and mind all of my fierce love, boundless energy, strength, and my expertise in the field of behavioral health and substance abuse. But I learned that love alone, a mother's fierce love, cannot heal an ill child, or a family fractured by that child's terminal illness of addiction.

All over the United States, fractured families similar to ours suffer tragically in part due to the impact of greed upon the human heart. With the relentless marketing and sales of Oxycontin, the Sackler family has profited from the suffering of thousands of families who are grieving the deaths of their loved ones to opioids.

The Sackler family owns Purdue Pharma, the pharmaceutical giant that makes the Oxycontin narcotic pill which is at the genesis of the worsening opiate overdose epidemic. This family has made profits of $4 billion in just over a decade from 2007 to 2017 on the sale of this narcotic. Purdue Pharma and leading Sackler family members are accused of deceiving the public and medical doctors about the addictive dangers of Oxycontin and are being sued on many fronts by city, county, and state authorities across the US (Joanna Walters, The Guardian, 2-1-19).

Chapter 7
SUDDEN ILLNESS

The folk saying which describes the weather for the month of March as "In like a lion, out like a lamb" is an apt description of the beginning of Ethan's life. Ethan was born March 6th, 1991, as the opioid crisis was being seeded in Ohio, Virginia, and Florida. He had a dominating physical presence even before he was born. He took over my body, and I gained over fifty-five pounds during my pregnancy. I was overwhelmed by the sheer size of this child coming out of my body into this world. The nurses said he looked like a three-month-old at birth! He had large blue eyes that intently held your gaze. He was a sunny, gregarious, quick-witted, sweet-tempered, and insatiably curious child. He was affectionate and loved giving and getting hugs and kisses. He needed lots of physical connection through roughhousing play and cuddling. I breastfed him until he was about eighteen months, as he didn't want to give up the soothing comfort of nursing. He followed his older sister everywhere, with his eyes at first, and then with his sturdy little legs. She was small and petite, and the two of them together were often mistaken to be twins until he was six and she was eight. He was willing to play whatever game she wanted, even playing "dress-up." We have photos of him festooned with necklaces, scarves, and tottering in high heels after his sister.

As he grew, it was apparent to us and his teachers that he was exceptionally bright, and so he was placed in a gifted and talented

program track in elementary school. He was competitive, and when he beat you at something, he did so with such delight that you couldn't help but be delighted for him, too. He liked predictability and familiarity in his daily life. He struggled with change. Starting with preschool, and for the rest of his schooling years even through college, the beginning of a school year or even a semester caused him to be off-kilter both emotionally and behaviorally for a while. Transitions in general were challenging for him to manage, such as the start or end of the day, or when it was time to stop playtime. He would not want to stop creating the complex cities he built full of roads for his Matchbox cars and fire trucks. He often procrastinated beginning a project or assignment.

He was a homebody, and due to the homesickness he felt when away from home, he rarely slept over at the homes of friends or even relatives. He was a very deep sleeper, prone to night terrors that would wake us all up in the middle of the night. He would whimper and scream, but would remember nothing in the morning. Due to his deep sleeping states, he continued bed-wetting until age thirteen, about which he felt embarrassed. His dad would matter-of-factly help Ethan strip the bed and change the sheets in the morning, reassuring him to not worry about it. As parents, we treated it as nothing to be ashamed about; we consulted with a urologist who said he was fine and would grow out of it. He reassured Ethan, "You will not walk down the aisle on your wedding day still wetting the bed," making Ethan burst out laughing.

His curiosity about the world was passionate and voracious. He asked questions about everything, starting so many conversations with "Why...?" His sister would roll her eyes in the back seat when he started chattering during car rides going just about anywhere. He read every *Harry Potter* book multiple times, collecting them all. He brought the whole series with him to college, saying when I protested that they would take up precious space in his dorm room,

"I just like having them around." As a teenager, he debated almost every rule and expectation we laid out for our children and energetically campaigned for his ideas and opinions to win out. When he was wrong, he was quick to wholeheartedly apologize. He was not one to hold a grudge; instead he forgave completely. He loved the

Los Angeles Lakers, and his hero was Kobe Bryant. He knew all of the Lakers' statistics by heart. He also was fascinated with crime statistics and could quote by memory the homicide rate of every major metropolitan area in the United States. I would quiz him just to see if I could name a city he didn't know. I always lost that contest.

Ethan was stubborn, and he knew he was very smart. These two aspects of him would prove to be his worst enemies in his recovery. He also tended toward some anxiety and often sought reassurance from us. He was terribly upset by the blooming acne on his face, anxiously scanning his face in every mirror in the house. He gravitated toward music: playing piano, learning percussion in an ensemble by audition-only. He took up playing guitar as he grew up watching his dad play and taught himself to play amazingly well, singing out earnestly with a strong voice as he played. In fact, he strode around the house as his body grew by inches and feet to well over six

feet tall by high school, usually belting out some song he was teaching himself, either Jason Mraz, Jack Johnson, or Ben Folds. I loved hearing him sing out loud, so full of uninhibited joy, the joy of a healthy teenage boy. He loved sports and played youth football and traveling basketball in middle school and ran cross country and track in high school, qualifying for the State meet his junior year. There seemed to be no endeavor that he would try and not achieve some measure of success.

Ethan was a leader and could be mischievous. His friend Kelly shared with me after he died that, "Ethan knew my house was close to school and suggested the team should run to my house during track practice instead of doing the long runs we were told to do by our coach. We followed him, played basketball, and drank Kool-Aid. It was super fun! Eventually, too many people came, and we all got caught for skipping our long runs. Ethan took all the responsibility for what we did."

Kelly also shared with me that, "Ethan told me a million things I had never heard of before. He was wicked smart. I was constantly in awe of everything he knew. He brought me out of my shy and sheltered shell. He teased me for absolutely everything, except he did not tease me at all when I went through the horrible and dark experience of wearing a back brace for scoliosis. Then, he told me I was attractive and beautiful."

Ethan was an empathic person and a good listener. His best friend from college, Kevin, said in his eulogy at Ethan's funeral, "Without Ethan's support during a difficult time of loss in my life, I don't know where I would be today."

Ethan woke up on a Saturday morning the third week into his senior year of high school saying he didn't feel right, that he felt as if there was a "black cloud over him." He had been pushed into a severe depression, as if he fell off a cliff, off of the edge of the stable ground of his passionate, funny, loving, and talented self. He quickly became sad, morose, anxiety-ridden, and seemed to be a shadow of his former self. Ethan had stopped a normal five-month course of Accutane, a drug prescribed for acne, a month before school started. Within six weeks, we brought him to a counselor, who after learning his history said that she was aware of a link between taking Accutane and serious depression in adolescents. We immediately began seeking ways to counteract what seemed to be a very serious side effect of his acne medication. We brought him to his primary care provider who prescribed antidepressants, which only made him feel suicidal. She prescribed anti-anxiety medications which he began abusing. One evening, arriving home for dinner, he staggered walking in the door and couldn't speak clearly. We rushed him to an emergency department where he was stabilized and released the next morning.

We monitored his medications after that scary event. This gave us a false sense of being able to prevent another overdose of his meds. However, what we couldn't control was what we didn't know. He began to use and abuse non-prescribed substances.

One evening during Christmas break of his senior year, he became combative and belligerent while having friends over. He threatened his dad with a hammer when Jeff told Ethan that his friends needed to leave. He began acting in a rage-fueled and almost psychotic way, walking up and down our street yelling. He refused to come back into the house. Jeff called the Greenfield Police, Jeff's own department, but they could not calm him down. Jeff looked at me with a question in his eyes, "What the hell do we do now?" I felt frozen, unable to process Ethan's surreal behavior unfolding in front of us. It was our daughter Deva, home from college for Christmas, who recognized the degree to which Ethan needed intervention.

She said, "Mom, he can't come back into this house. He isn't safe to be around, and he may not be safe with himself." She told us that we had to bring him to a hospital right away, because he was behaving in such a threatening way: refusing to calm down, refusing or unable to listen to anyone, refusing to take his prescribed psychiatric medications. Deva's calm, clear manner and her astute assessment of the situation lifted me out of my frozen state. Her wisdom at that frightening moment foreshadowed her skill as a psychotherapist. I remember thinking later how powerful trauma is: my feelings of being so scared and stunned by Ethan's behavior completely shut down my cognitive knowledge as a psychotherapist to the degree that I literally could not see my way through to a plan of action. That night marked the beginning of Deva shifting her relationship with her brother from that of normal siblings to one where she worried about him almost like another parent.

Ethan refused to be voluntarily hospitalized. We later learned that he had been drinking bottles of Robitussin cough syrup. After being discharged, he cooperatively completed a step-down partial hospitalization program. His psychiatrist sought to try to find medication that would help mitigate his crushing depression and worsening anxiety. Ethan thankfully welcomed our involvement in treatment.

Shortly after he was discharged in January of 2009, he competed in the Whitnall High School talent show and won for his piano solo of "Landed" by Ben Folds and his guitar solo of "The Remedy" by Jason Mraz. The passion and power of his performances that night were beautiful to watch. We left the auditorium that night whispering to each other, "Maybe Ethan is back to his happy, healthy self!"

However, the remainder of his senior year was marked by his intermittent difficulty attending classes or even attending school at all. In the spring, he decided to drop out of the track team to try to focus on his schoolwork from home. Jeff stayed home from his job as a detective many days that spring when Ethan could not stay in school.

Ethan attempted suicide within a few days of graduating from high school. Fear settled deep inside us as we saw him getting inexplicably worse to the point of wanting to take his own life. We were confused by his worsening depression despite being on medications and participating in individual and family therapy. It was the most frightening thing we had ever experienced as parents thus far. Little did we know that this was going to get much, much worse.

Most heroin addicts begin their drug abuse with opioid painkillers like oxycodone, either prescribed to them legally, or obtained from others

who were oversupplied, stolen from family or friends, or from criminal diversion from pharmacies through fraud.

Ethan went away to Carthage College in Kenosha, Wisconsin despite his therapist's suggestion that he live at home and attend an Extension of the University of Wisconsin system in the nearby suburb of Waukesha, just for the first year due to his recent hospitalization. He insisted that he wanted to go away to college. We didn't stand in the way of his decision, despite our misgivings. He was successful at Carthage, getting almost a 4.0 average and majoring in chemistry. He remained in therapy voluntarily with his therapist from high school and seemed to benefit from it to manage his depression and anxiety. He maintained that year, whenever we asked, that he was clean from any substance abuse. We began to feel that perhaps he was truly going to be okay. After his freshman year, he decided he didn't like the "small town" feel of Carthage, and insisted on transferring three hours away to a large school, the University of Wisconsin-La Crosse. The environment of this public school was much less protective than that of Carthage, a small private school. Ethan's transfer marked the beginning of his prodigious drug use, something we didn't learn until his junior year.

Due to his distance from home, we encouraged him to establish relationships with health care providers in La Crosse. He did so, obtaining a primary care doctor and a psychotherapist who specialized in substance abuse. He also sought out care from orthopedic providers there. This proved to be a terrible mistake, as he was prescribed Vicodin, Oxycontin, and Oxycodone for pain from old sports injuries, new back pain, new knee pain, and new hip pain by these orthopedic providers. We had no knowledge of this. In addition, after getting his wisdom teeth extracted, he was prescribed Percocet.

He developed an addiction to these opiates, seemingly legitimately prescribed to him, that we only became aware of two years later when he attempted suicide again. We raced up to La Crosse that weekend after Father's Day to meet him in the hospital. He was stabilized medically and then transferred to a behavioral health inpatient unit, where a psychiatrist trained in addictionology suspected some drug dependency and did a complete drug and alcohol assessment on our son. To our shock and dismay, Ethan admitted to abusing opiates and many other street drugs as well, in addition to binge drinking.

He came home to live with us for the summer, quitting his summer job in La Crosse, and received treatment in a Dual Diagnosis program for his depression and substance use disorder. One day, he called both of us at work and urgently asked us to meet him for an emergency session with his long-term therapist. There, he told us he had met a girl in the Dual Diagnosis program who had introduced him to heroin. He admitted to using heroin for the past month, draining his whole savings account of $1,200 on buying heroin. Hearing this in the therapist's office, I said the word "fuck" for the first time in my life out of a mixture of anger and a deep fear that Ethan was getting worse again, not better.

He said he wanted help and seemed full of motivation to kick the heroin. He lived at home that fall, taking a class at the University of Wisconsin-Milwaukee so as not to get behind in his studies. He agreed to be admitted into the Opiate Recovery program in the health care organization I was working for at the time. He immediately began partial hospitalization, which was full day programming seven days a week for several weeks. He then stepped down into Intensive Outpatient programming, followed by individual care with the program psychiatrist who prescribed Suboxone, a form of Medication Assisted Treatment (MAT). MAT is strongly indicated for the treatment of opiate addiction. He did well and, when seemingly stable, returned to school in La Crosse in January of 2014 to complete his last three semesters.

He successfully graduated from college with honors in December of 2014. I was tearful with a mixture of joy, pride, and relief! I had feared he would die before he graduated from college. He remained living in La Crosse and working. However, without the structure of college life, he relapsed within two months, and within four months of graduation, he was regularly using heroin again. We supported him to get into treatment in La Crosse, working with him via long-distance family phone sessions with a therapist in La Crosse. He was luckily able to get a bed in a month-long Residential Treatment facility there. We had high hopes that this safe and sheltering environment would anchor a sustained recovery practice for Ethan, such as going to meetings, getting a sponsor, and no longer living with roommates who drank. He stayed only for one week, deciding to leave against medical advice because he felt he could do this on his own. He didn't explain his decision or answer our frantic phone calls to him. It was a devastating blow to get that call on a Tuesday evening from the staff at the facility informing us that Ethan had left AMA. They told us he would not be allowed to return.

We had, at this time, been walking this agonizing journey with him for almost seven years. We couldn't make any sense of his decision to leave a program that had huge potential to help him in his efforts to be free of what he, in his own words, labeled, "being shackled to heroin." We were overwhelmed with utter helplessness, frustration, and fear. We felt fear that he would die if he didn't stay in treatment. We felt helpless that we couldn't stop his rollercoaster of sobriety, relapse, sobriety, relapse. We felt angry and frustrated with him that he had rejected an opportunity to get clean.

It was at this juncture that I knew I needed to step back and not work so hard at trying to pour into him my motivation and my desire for him to get clean. I kept pouring love into him, but if I didn't step back with the other pieces, I was going to start losing myself. And so, I did step back. When he reached out for support from us moving forward from that time, I asked him, "What do *you* think you need to do for *you*?" He decided twice to check himself into an inpatient psychiatric hospital in La Crosse when he felt suicidal, rather than hurting himself. He even made these self-care decisions on his own, as we were traveling in Italy at the time. We were proud of his choices and gave him lots of positive feedback, as did his girlfriend Ariana.

After his death, when I read the treatment notes from those two hospital stays, I saw that the inpatient therapist tried to solicit over and over again Ethan's thoughts about why his depression was so persistent. Ethan kept repeating to the therapist, "I don't know."

His words resonated with me. Over the years it seemed that Ethan's depression, which seemed to overtake him as a seventeen-year-old boy as a side effect of Accutane, had grown entangled with his substance abuse as an adult man. It was confusing to us, and many of his providers, as to what was driving this reality. As a therapist, I believe that we may not understand *how* something got so bad until we move past it and can look back on it. Insight can sometimes be attained in hindsight.

PART TWO

Chapter 8
PSYCHOLOGICAL AUTOPSY

An intense need to better understand why my son died began to overtake me in the first weeks after Ethan's death. I still believed in the very deepest part of me that with all of the treatment, resources, and support that Ethan had available to him that he... Should. Not. Have. Died. How could this outcome have happened? I relentlessly searched for clues of who he was at the end of his life. He had received treatment at the four best behavioral health systems in Wisconsin and had expert, caring providers. He had been raised in a loving, supportive, and church-going family. He had a healthy girlfriend who was supportive of his recovery, a mother and a sister who are both in the behavioral health field, and a loving father who was a police officer. How could he not have survived his illness? Did we not say enough prayers, or not the right prayers? My search to make sense of this outcome belied my professional belief that addiction can grab hold of any one of us despite all of those protective factors.

A person with the illness of addiction is always either moving toward death or toward recovery. I discovered in my exploration of Ethan's last months that he had been moving toward death for quite a while—unknown to us, his sister, or even his girlfriend.

As a family, we attended the appointment Ethan had scheduled with his therapist in La Crosse for December 30th, 2016, to glean any information that could shed light on what went awry in his recovery. We told her about the wonderful Christmas we had with him, his desire to address his excessive drinking, and his willingness to reconnect with his sponsor. Tearfully, we described the horror of finding him dead of a suspected overdose. She shared with us that he had reached out to her on December 6th, 2016, saying in his voicemail to her that he had relapsed on heroin while home for Thanksgiving and needed an urgent appointment. She called him back within the hour and offered a same-day appointment, but she never heard back from him.

We despaired to learn that Ethan did not attend any appointments the month of December, and, in fact, he had only actually kept two appointments with her since his intake with her in October. She shared, "There was something so compelling about Ethan's dogged efforts to keep rescheduling his missed appointments with me. So, I broke our agency's rule of discharging after two missed appointments and gave him extra chances. He seemed so determined to try to work on his addiction." The juxtaposition of reaching out toward help and then withdrawing from using that help is a maddening and sometimes lethal cycle that a person with an opiate addiction can suffer from.

Science has maintained that energy does not die but merely changes its form from an Earthly body to an energetic form. Socrates wrote that death is the release of our soul or our spirit from "the chains of the body." This must have been true for Ethan. It must have been a sweet relief for his spirit to be free from the cravings and depression that gnawed at him. His body and mind grew increasingly shackled to the need for opiates in the last three months of his life, with methadone no longer present in his brain to mitigate the cravings. We learned that he had refused his therapist's suggestions to try either Vivitrol or go back on Suboxone, both also effective MAT types for opiate addiction.

We had visited him in October, per our usual visiting schedule with him every two months. We spoke very plainly to him then and emphasized that while it was his decision if he was going to pursue treatment or not, we needed to protect ourselves from the intense worry and fear we felt that he might relapse and die if he wasn't in treatment. We told him he couldn't come home for Thanksgiving if he wasn't in treatment. This had been a decision we had agonized over making as we prepared to visit him in October. He decided to go to an assessment appointment while we were still there. He was referred to a substance abuse counselor, and he assured us he would be following up with her.

The grief counselor whom I saw after Ethan died described the end of my son's life as being in "the later stages of a terminal illness."

I would find myself for months after Ethan's death suddenly thinking, "Oh, I have to tell Ethan about…" a recovery idea, or a group, or a treatment program I came across. I would literally shake myself, groaning out loud, "He doesn't need any of those things anymore. He is gone." Those flashes of ideas to help Ethan were the dying embers of the fire deep within my heart and soul, that fueled my energy and love toward helping Ethan get well and supporting him moving toward recovery for all of those years. It took a long, long time for that heat to completely extinguish.

During the week I spent alone after Ethan's funeral, I read the Narcotics Anonymous book of recovery stories I had just given him for Christmas. I read story after story of courageous people who managed to find recovery and sustained it. I recognized Ethan in many of their stories, particularly one titled "Academic Addict," who reminded me of Ethan with his encyclopedic knowledge of drugs and their pharmacological properties. This recovering man wrote, "My key delusion was that my problem only involved me; either I could solve it, or no one could. My isolation paved the road to active addiction, and it nearly killed me." His comment made me recall once when Ethan told me about why he didn't like to go to meetings; he said he felt "aloof" when he was in a meeting. In my interviews of many who interacted with Ethan in those last months, I gradually learned how Ethan kept secrets and isolated himself, even from his girlfriend.

Grasping to try to understand Ethan's addiction from the inside out, I seriously contemplated trying a prescription pain killer myself and even trying heroin. I didn't have the energy to obtain either. Instead, I turned to reading for understanding what that experience would be like, as I have done my whole life. I read *Portrait of an Addict as a Young Man*, by Bill Clegg, who graphically describes his descent into the hell of addiction, and his follow-up memoir of recovery, *Ninety Days*, in which he describes his journey toward successful recovery by committing to the classic "ninety meetings in ninety days" strategy. I read *Chasing the Scream: The First and Last Days of the War on Drugs* and became depressed by the research that connects drug addiction with childhood trauma. Ethan was not raised in a traumatic environment...or did we maybe do something to him that we didn't realize as parents? I read *Dreamland*, the story of the seeds and the spread of the opiate epidemic in this country. I read *Unbroken Brain* by Maia Szalavitz, a recovered heroin and cocaine addict, who outlines her premise that addiction is a developmental disorder, specifically a learning disorder. She challenges the concept that addicts have a "broken brain" or an "addictive personality." She describes addiction, instead, as a behavior that is learned, and can also be unlearned with proper treatment (which support groups by themselves are not). She published this in 2016, too late for Ethan to benefit from her theories. I felt burdened with another layer of grief as I asked myself over and over: had I—or, we as parents—done something that caused Ethan's addiction? Or, *not* done something that could have helped him stay alive? Had Ethan received the treatment he *needed* from his providers, not just the treatment that was *available?* Was there more I could have done to find better treatment, or treatment that would have stuck with him, or treatment that he would have been willing to commit to?

Determined to find answers to these questions, I signed releases for and obtained Ethan's medical records from every medical and behavioral health hospital and clinic he had received treatment from over the last eight years of his life. I read thousands of notes on paper and digitally on CDs. My questions appeared to be a consistent theme that his providers wrestled with themselves. Je-Mae helped me with a review of voluminous documentation from a facility in La Crosse where he received behavioral health outpatient, inpatient, and stepdown care in multiple treatment episodes. One of Ethan's documented strengths was that he kept returning to treatment to try again. He also received medical care in this same system from a primary care provider and orthopedic providers. It was clear from the notes that these medical and orthopedic providers did *not* communicate with the behavioral health side, a serious concern when that patient suffers from addiction.

She and I sat huddled together in front of a computer screen for five hours, not moving from our seats, drawn in by the story the notes were revealing. The notes from this system in La Crosse were the hardest to read of all the documentation I obtained. Ethan wanted us involved in his treatment as an adolescent, and even as a young adult in college, but our involvement appropriately lessened as we encouraged him to take responsibility for his own treatment after he graduated from college. Thus, I was not aware of the amount or frequency of his opiate prescriptions, despite the documented re-luctance on the part of these providers to continue to prescribe these drugs for his pain. Debilitating anxiety throughout his college years was also documented, as was his depression. We knew about these mental health issues; we had spent a lot of time on the phone with him those years while he was at college in La Crosse helping him through bouts of depression and anxiety. Our support of him as par-ents was positively documented in the notes, as well as his worry that his "problems" were causing us stress in our marriage. I cried when I read this; I thought we had successfully hidden this from him.

These were also the years that his polysubstance use skyrock-eted. We did not know about his drug use, though I suspected it at times when I was on the phone with him and could hear in his voice a strange difference that chilled me…he always denied my observation, saying, "Mom, you worry too much."

I found shocking evidence to the contrary in Ethan's own words, in his own handwriting, from his treatment journal during the one week he was in the residential treatment program for his opiate/heroin addiction. He wrote pages of meticulously clear, hon-est documentation as he worked through the first three steps of the Twelve-Step program. Reading his honest accounting of the vast array and amounts of drugs he had used since high school was so upsetting to me that I vomited the first time I read it. But the truth shone through in his words, and I could imagine hearing his deep voice speaking them. Ethan wrote, "I was faded, fucked up, high, so many times over the years…I spent thousands on drugs, I stole money from my parents and a best friend to buy drugs. I've called in sick many times because of my drug use…My addiction has made me at times very complacent about my job at Jimmy Johns for the past three years, and more importantly, about not beginning to look for a better job, or even starting to develop a career for myself."

Ethan's insightful choice of the word "complacent" struck me only when I read his words again three years after he died. I looked it up: Merriam-Webster's definition is "marked by self-satisfaction especially when accompanied by unawareness of actual dangers or deficiencies." Ethan wrote his words six months after he graduated from college. By his own admission, he seemed quite aware of the dangers of his drug use and the deficiencies it created in him. His words confirmed our observation that although he could demonstrate insight, his actual behavior was hijacked by his serious opiate addiction.

Another concerning discovery was the amount of benzodiazepines Ethan was prescribed in the last ninety days of his life. I called and spoke to his primary care provider in La Crosse about my concerns that he had prescribed benzodiazepines, which are addictive medications, for the debilitating insomnia Ethan suffered from when he went off of methadone ninety days before he died. Insomnia is a common side effect of methadone cessation. The doctor listened to my concern that Ethan's electronic medical record was not transparent about his opiate addiction diagnosis. I told Ethan's doctor how during the last month of his life he was successfully able to obtain several prescriptions for codeine cough syrup by going to Urgent Care and faking bronchitis symptoms. His primary doctor was not aware of Ethan's drug-seeking behavior. Trying not to sound blaming, though I felt that way, I urged his primary care provider to campaign for complete transparency in listing Substance Use Disorder diagnoses within their medical record. If in December the Urgent Care providers could have seen Ethan's addiction history in the record, which was well documented by his primary care doctor, they could have perhaps compassionately helped Ethan to see his behavior as drug-seeking and needing addiction treatment, not bronchitis treatment.

I also called and spoke to the managers of the two jobs he held in the last months of his life. I learned that he hadn't worked longer than a month as a server at a Buffalo Wild Wings restaurant. This was a surprise because Ethan had excitedly called us soon after getting this job saying, "Mom and Dad, I am making some serious coin here, and I like this job. I'm really good with the customers!" Ethan told us at Christmas that he left due to not getting enough scheduled hours. What his shift manager told me was that Ethan requested several times to leave before his shift ended; once she suspected he "faked an ankle sprain" in order to leave early, so she stopped giving him hours because she didn't view him as reliable. When I spoke to the general store manager, he told me he "observed how personable Ethan was with the customers, how well he connected with them." He told me he had reached out several times to Ethan after he quit but got no response.

More heartbreakingly, I learned when speaking to the manager of his new job as a Compliance Coordinator that he only worked two days. On his first day at his new job on December 5th, he reported two hours late, and the second day he arrived six hours late and then never went back. Listening to her recount this information in her kind voice, I couldn't take it in. I asked her again, "What do you mean, he never went back? He told us at Christmas he liked his job and that everyone was very nice!" This was the double life that Ethan was living. Speaking softly, she said that he finally called her on December 14th to say that he was "very sick" and couldn't work. She encouraged him to bring in a work excuse from his doctor and she would assist him in finding another opening within the company once he got well.

She said, "I really wanted to help Ethan join our company. He was so enthusiastic. I really liked how polite and well-spoken he was." She went on to say, "I could see how smart he was, he asked me great questions. I saw in him a lot of potential to succeed within our company."

I thought to myself, of course you did! Ethan was amazing! He was charming and could engage with anyone. He actually was quite ill, but not in the way he told you he was ill.

I decided to be open with her and told her that Ethan had a severe opiate addiction and died from an overdose just after Christmas.

She expressed sympathy, and then unbelievably went on to say, "You know, there are now so many drug addicts in La Crosse, that me and my husband are thinking of moving our family out of the area."

I was silent on the phone, wishing now that I had not been so open. I don't think she understood the judgment of "addicts" she just laid at my feet. One of those "addicts" had been my son. She added that she scheduled an appointment with him on December 21st to discuss other employment options, but he didn't keep the appointment, and she didn't hear from him again. That was two days before he came home for Christmas.

When I shared this information with his girlfriend, she was aghast. She said that she had no idea he had barely started his job and then never went back. She did remember, however, that once in mid-December she had questioned him about why he wasn't at work. He told her that, "My supervisor is on maternity leave, and they can't find a replacement for her so they told me not to go in." She thought that was kind of strange, but like us as parents, she was weary of always quizzing him when something didn't seem to add up, so she let it go. She told me that being the "truth police" with him was damaging their relationship.

I decided to call one of his four roommates and asked him how

Ethan seemed in December. He described being upset with Ethan for stealing his change and drinking his milk in the fridge. He said Ethan seemed to be home a lot in December always with some story about why he wasn't at work, bringing pizza and beer back to the apartment many nights, staying up late drinking and watching TV alone. This confirmed my suspicion that Ethan had been in a major relapse during the last thirty days of his life.

I also called Ethan's sponsor, Chris, whom Ethan had introduced us to during one of our visits to La Crosse. Chris was an older guy, thirty years in recovery from heroin addiction. Chris said that unfortunately he had not heard from Ethan in a long time, until he received Ethan's call on December 27th asking to get together with him the following Saturday for lunch. He was very sorry to hear of Ethan's death and said, "I really liked Ethan a lot, but I could see that Ethan struggled a lot with commitment to treatment." I agreed, and then asked him why he thought that was the case. He didn't have an answer for me.

Still trying to find more clues, I searched through all of the pieces of his life I could lay my eyes and hands on. I combed through the boyhood mementos in his bedroom at home that he had left behind when he moved to La Crosse. Normal boyhood trinkets, medals, photos, a Game Boy. Nothing portentous pertaining to the devastation that lay ahead in his life. I examined every scrap of paper from his room in La Crosse that we brought back to our house when we boxed up his things after his death. I did this with JeMae, as I didn't think I could bear doing this part of my searching alone. We found receipts for fast food, cards he had saved from his last birthday; we found unpaid bills for his school loans, invoices for unpaid rent, and a small credit card balance. Nothing that couldn't have been solved had he been honest with us or someone—anyone—about his relapsing.

In my darkest moments of grief, a thought I tried to keep buried deep inside of me came bubbling up, hissing, "This is what I deserve for all of the wrongs I have done in my life. My son is dead. Someone, or something, is to blame...and it is ME." The sea of my grief was contaminated by blame. My thought flowed like filthy water over my consciousness. That thought led to worse thoughts: "God, why did You let Ethan die and not the dealer that sold the heroin to him? You could have revived him in his car that night, or caused someone to see his slumped body in his car, bang on his window, and call for help...why did You let *ETHAN's* life drain away?" God says in Isaiah 43:2, "When you go through deep waters, I will be with you. When you go through rivers of difficulty, you will not drown." I felt God had betrayed his promise to me. I was engulfed in blame.

But, blaming myself and God gave me no peace.

I drove to the McDonald's parking lot where he died. There, I tried to listen for Ethan, to feel his presence. I pleaded with him to help me understand how he could have died after so much treatment, support, prayers, and love from so many. I parked there a dozen times as winter softened into a blooming spring, and summer burst forth. The seasons moved along in their rhythm indifferent to my searching for answers—some meager relief from my pain. I parked there with Jeff, with Deva, and Ethan's girlfriend when she visited from Minneapolis. I felt raw and flayed open with others there, so I began going alone. I would be irritated when I pulled in and someone would be parked in the parking space where he died; how dare they park there? Once parked, I would sit very still with my eyes closed, my gaze turned inward. Sometimes, my eyes stayed open, roving for a sign from Ethan. He was never there. I never felt him. Sitting there sometimes caused me to relive the awful scene of the night he died. I tried to hold the images at bay, but they took over my mind—the hulk of the fire truck and police squad cars, the lights flashing, the broken glass…it felt surreal sitting there in the daytime with the sunshine flooding my car, no emergency scene unfolding in the parking lot, only unfolding again and again in my mind. Gradually, I went less and less and finally stopped going altogether.

I see now that I was looking for a rational answer to an irrational act. My incessant searching was for an answer that could make some meaning out of the horror of the ending of my son's life. Doing what amounted to an autopsy of my son's life did not give me the meaning I was searching for, nor the relief from the pain of grieving the loss of Ethan in my life. I was looking to understand what I much later came to accept as an error—albeit, a lethal error—of judgement on Ethan's part. His error of thinking that he could use the same amount of heroin that he used before he was on methadone for nineteen months. That he could snort heroin in a parking lot on his way out of town after a wonderful Christmas visit with his family and drive away from that parking lot alive. That he could use heroin after calling his girlfriend and still plan to arrive alive in La Crosse three hours later. This error in Ethan's judgement was a result of the disease of addiction, not a lack of morals or a character flaw on his part.

For many months after Ethan's death, I spoke periodically with the kind-hearted detective from the Brookfield Police Department who was assigned to Ethan's case. Ethan's death was linked with several other area overdose deaths, all connected by the same drug dealer's phone number showing up in the cell phones of the deceased young victims. I checked in regularly for any progress on the case, but there was not enough evidence to move forward with a prosecution, as more evidence was needed from Ethan's cell phone. His phone unfortunately lost power before we could figure out what his passcode was to unlock it. His phone is still in holding as evidence at the Brookfield Police Department.

I am aware that the dealer that sold Ethan's last heroin bag to him may even now still be selling to other desperate users addicted to heroin. I had to eventually release my hope that the dealer who sold Ethan his last bag of heroin would be punished for his death. Release my hope that he or she would at least suffer for Ethan's death. Release my desire to blame the dealer. Release my hope that I could point to that person and say, "You caused my son's death."

I gradually came to understand that what took Ethan's life was simply—and terribly—the incredibly complex disease of addiction that engulfed him again after he went off methadone. I came to acknowledge that the dealer may have sold Ethan heroin to fuel their own addiction.

Any anger I had toward Ethan from all those years had drained away in my long months of searching for clues. Love and deep compassion for him remained. Nothing to forgive. He was very ill at the end of his life, and he chose not to tell anyone really how ill he was. He made that decision, likely out of a desire to protect those whom he loved. I'm certain he didn't think he was going to die that day when he used heroin at the end of his Christmas visit with his family.

He was tragically and irrevocably wrong.

Chapter 9
SEARCHING AND
MORE SEARCHING

What I didn't know was that forgiving *myself* was going to take me more than the next two years of my life to accomplish.

As a psychotherapist, I deeply believe in the healing power of therapy, so I quickly began seeing a grief counselor after Ethan's death. She confirmed for me that my searching for answers for why Ethan died was a normal part of grieving such a traumatic loss. She observed how much I was also yearning for a connection with Ethan. She surprised me with a suggestion that I consult a medium, one who serves as a voice for those who no longer have a physical voice. I am trained as a cognitive behavioral psychotherapist, and I was skeptical that a medium was a legitimate thing. I did some research and learned that a medium has the gift of communicating with spirits, in addition to their psychic abilities. I learned that psychics are not fortune tellers, but are persons who are highly attuned to being able to read a person's energy and tell them things about themselves that they may be aware of only at a subconscious or unconscious level. I am now convinced that authentic mediums are truly blessed with the remarkable ability to relay messages from a deceased person's spirit to their loved one here on Earth, should that spirit be willing to present themselves.

Despite my initial skepticism, I was willing to try anything to connect with Ethan. I scheduled an appointment with a medium named Stacey and then waited two long weeks. I wanted to cancel when the appointment arrived, exhausted from my work day. For some reason, I couldn't follow through with cancelling, and so I kept my appointment. I found myself in a serene office, sitting across from an ordinary woman wearing jeans and a plaid shirt. Per her website instructions, I brought a photo of Ethan with his eyes looking directly out from the photo. I handed it to her, and she asked me his first name but nothing more as to his relationship to me. Stacey explained that she was going to ask his spirit to be present and to communicate with us. She asked that I remain calm and quiet, and that I try not to judge or analyze what she would relate to me from the spirit communication. She instructed me to simply listen. She invited me to record the session, but I declined. She then closed her eyes, tilted her head to one side, and sat very still for a few moments.

Opening her eyes, she said, "Ethan is standing right by you on your left side, with his hand on your left shoulder. Do you feel him?"

I said, "No, I don't." I wanted to, very badly, but I honestly did not.

She warmly chuckled, and said, "He is very eager to talk to you, but a woman is pushing past him in line. She is a tiny thing with white hair. She's a spitfire! She has an open, kind face. She has sparkling eyes behind glasses, and a charming smile, with dimples. Do you know who this is?"

I breathed, "Yes! That is my Nana!" I smiled in spite of myself to hear that my paternal grandmother, all four foot eleven inches of her, was pushing past my six foot plus tall son.

Stacey said, "She wants you to know that she has great love for you. She is watching over you, and is very concerned about you."

I nodded, suddenly feeling tearful as I received this message of love from my Nana.

Stacey said, "Ethan seems to be communicating as your son, does this make sense to you?"

I nodded, "Yes."

She said, "He is standing next to a large dog that is very lean and darkish with a mottled coat, and he is holding a small dog with a white coat."

I thought with wonder to myself that the large dog must be Ethan's favorite greyhound, Mo, his favorite of our five greyhounds we adopted over the years. The small dog must be the shih tzu we adopted when he was in high school—the dog he insisted on naming Kobe after his favorite basketball player, Kobe Bryant.

She then said, "Ethan says he has seen the baby, and the baby is fine."

I was confused; who could he be talking about?

Seeing my puzzlement, she said, "Did you have a baby that died?"

I froze, and then answered, "Actually, yes, my first pregnancy ended in a miscarriage." I thought, Oh my goodness, could Ethan really have met our unborn baby? His sibling?

"Ethan is telling you," Stacey said, 'I get it now, Mom, why you talked to me so much about God. I understand now.'" She told me that Ethan was "very active in the spirit world," and that he seems to be "a bit of a smart ass, sarcastic, playful, calling you 'Ma' even though he knows you don't like to be called that name."

I nodded, smiling, tears starting to well up in my eyes again. I hadn't expected to feel happy during this meeting!

She went on to say, "Ethan doesn't want to talk about how he died, but he is saying this: 'I'm so sorry, Mom, that you and Dad had to find my body in the way you did. When you guys found me, I was already long gone, I just went to sleep. I'm at peace now.'"

I caught my breath, holding back a sob. This apology was just like Ethan, to be sensitive to what that experience was like for his dad and me. I closed my eyes, so I could imprint his words, his deep voice saying these words, in my head. I wanted to share this with his dad. Another gift from Ethan. An angry thought rose up in me, "I'm so glad you are at peace, Ethan, but we surely are not down here." I quickly tried to quash that thought, as it felt selfish.

Stacey said to me, "He tries to reach out to you, but can't get through to you because you are shrouded as if by a grey mist." I was startled to hear the word "shrouded" as this was the word Ethan used repeatedly to describe how he felt when he was depressed.

The medium continued sharing more of Ethan's spirit communication. She said, "Ethan appeared at the foot of the bed of someone you know, Robin, and Ethan says you must believe the message that he gave to this person for you." I froze again—how could she know about Ethan's appearance in Radhe's bedroom just after he died? Could this really be Ethan's spirit in this office?

"Ethan also tells me that he was recently with you and his dad when you two were sitting around a round table quietly sharing memories of him."

My mind immediately spooled back two weeks earlier when Jeff and I were sitting around a small round high-top table at the top floor of a hotel in downtown Chicago. It was midday, the room was full of sunshine, and we were overlooking the blue expanse of Lake Michigan. We were waiting for someone, and while waiting, we slowly began to share memories of taking Ethan and his sister Deva to Chicago every Christmas as a family once they became teenagers. We had laughed together as we remembered our family's fun experiences going to an earsplitting Trans-Siberian Orchestra concert and our extensive exploration of the Chicago Aquarium. Our conversation at that round table was probably the first positive conversation Jeff and I had in the ninety days since Ethan died. Had Ethan really been there at that table sitting with us while we reminisced? My mind struggled to comprehend how Ethan could be with us as a spirit…I didn't feel him that day, or even now, as she continued to speak.

"Ethan says you are stubborn and will not listen to him telling you to let him go. While he appreciates the place you have in your home where you display many photos, belongings, and mementos of Ethan, he is telling you that you don't need these things to remember him by." Lastly, Stacey said, "Ethan is telling me that you have a journal of his that you need to read. It will help you to understand better why he died." I nodded, instantly remembering my shock when I started reading his treatment journal just weeks earlier.

My meeting with the medium ended. The sixty minutes felt like one long inhaling breath, trying to breathe in the reality of Ethan's spirit—and one long exhaling breath trying to let go of blaming myself for Ethan's death.

I returned home and tried to stay connected to my joy in this miraculous communication with Ethan's spirit. But my joy was too fragile. Blame seeped back in, covering my momentary elation.

At the advice of my friend JeMae, I read *Radical Forgiveness* by Colin Tipping in an effort to expand my ability to truly forgive myself. I gleaned from my reading that we are to learn something important from our struggles. What was I meant to learn from this wrenching experience of trying to forgive myself? I did as many heart-opening yoga poses as I could. I wanted my heart to open wide to allow in healing. I prayed and prayed. I appealed to God to help me release my blame.

"In desperate hope I go and search for her in all the corners of my house. I find her not. My house is small and what once has gone from it can never be regained. But infinite is thy mansion, my Lord, and in seeking her I have come to Thy door. I stand under the golden canopy of your evening sky and I lift my eager eyes to thy face…Oh, dip my emptied life into that ocean, plunge it into the deepest fullness. Let me

for once feel that lost sweet touch in the allness of the universe." —from *Gitanjali*, a collection of poetry by Rabindranath Tagore, 1910

I was not released. Despite my efforts and prayers, I continued to deeply blame myself for how I handled the conversation Jeff and I had with Ethan the day after Christmas 2016. I replayed that conversation dozens of times in my head, imagining what I could have said to have encouraged Ethan to open up and reveal to us while still alive what we would learn shortly after his death: that he had been relapsing, that there was no new job, no engagement in counseling, and he was, in fact, going to be evicted in four days. I see myself in my mind's eye, setting aside my motherly confusion, calmly putting on my therapist hat, and asking neutral curious questions, such as, "Hmm, that is a surprising request, Ethan, can you say more about that? What are your thoughts about how that would be helpful to you? What would be your plan, should you move here, to not contact your Milwaukee dealers?" And so on, and so on…I have conjured up whole sessions worth of therapeutic dialogue that ends with Ethan telling us his true situation every time I unravel it. Ethan is honest with us in our living room about his dire circumstances of not being able to work and having no money; he admits to us that he has been drinking and abusing opiates since Thanksgiving, and that he wants help. We work with him to get him into a partial hospitalization program that very day. He never leaves the house with his dad's twenty dollar bill in his wallet. And he *lives*.

I returned to the medium six weeks later. As those early months ground on, I continued to yearn for connection with Ethan.

I told Stacey that I was tormented by the last conversation with my son the night before he died in which I felt I had failed him. She listened to me recount the story of this conversation. She calmly said, "Nothing you could have done or said would have made a difference in the end of his life."

I became very still as I listened to her words, trying to accept this as truth.

She said, "I sense a deep darkness and depression within Ethan that he struggled to understand and cope with. Ethan struggled to acknowledge how smart and gifted he was; he was quick to judge himself. He took people's behavior towards him very personally, and he was easily hurt."

I understood this. Those qualities can be the painful cost of being a sensitive person.

Stacey said, "You and Ethan are soul mates. He is now trying to teach you to not judge yourself." Gently she went on to say, "Ethan was not meant to be on this earth for long. He was here as long as he was because of you and his father's extraordinary love and support of him. Robin, you have known on a soul level for a long time that Ethan would die before you." My heart was pierced with the deep knowing of this truth I had inside of me, as it rose to the surface of my consciousness.

I thought about her words as I drove away from her office, aimlessly meandering, not wanting to go home. I stopped in a park and started walking, even though I could smell a spring thunderstorm building after days of steamy weather. I was too far from my car to get back when the sky cracked open and driving rain and wind swirled around me. I ran to the park pavilion and stood there watching the power of the wind tossing about the stout tree limbs, the rain cascading off of the pavilion roof in a torrent, the lightening crackling in the sky. I shouted out loud, "God, you have all of this mighty power! You could have averted Ethan's death if you saw fit to save him! Was he not worth saving? You could have extended his time here on earth! Why have you rained down upon me and my family the terrible loss of our son and brother? Why, why, WHY?"

It was a long time in my journey before I learned that these were completely futile questions to ask. These were not the questions that would lead me toward peace. These questions only led me down a path of disconnection from God and disconnection from myself.

Ethan's spring birthday drew near. A robin began visiting our home. He—I wanted to believe it was a "he"—perched on the window box outside our family room window and pecked determinedly at the glass. Watching the bird, I asked, "Ethan, is that you? If that is you, Ethan, you don't need to peck so insistently and beat your wings so forcefully; this is your home!"

He visited our home for about two weeks. I hoped in my heart that this spring robin was Ethan's spirit, wanting to be with us as we awkwardly and painfully tried to celebrate with close friends and family what would have been Ethan's 26th birthday. Shortly after Ethan's birthday was over, the robin was gone. I missed his tapping and flapping.

Jeff also left our home by Ethan's birthday. He began living with a friend.

Chapter 10
SHROUDED

"Rather than a human on a spiritual path,
we are spirit discovering itself through human interaction."
— True Refuge, Tara Brach

As the months wore on, I gradually crumbled, losing pieces of myself. I lost weight steadily, without any awareness it was occurring. I recall teaching a yoga class during that time and as I was demonstrating a seated twist, I stopped in mid-cue, as I felt my right hand land on a sharp plane of bone on my left hip. Confused, I thought, "What's that? Have I injured myself?" I grasped the plane of bone and realized that it was my own hip, unfamiliar and strange in its sharpness. It felt vulnerable to me, as though it needed comfort. I almost started to cry, feeling grief for my own disembodied self.

I didn't feel much hunger or thirst. Strangely, I could only eat five things: bananas, spinach, hard boiled eggs, cottage cheese, and Goldfish crackers. A lifelong athlete, I typically had a connection to my body and listened to it. I lost that ability after Ethan died. I also lost my interest in reading fiction, a lifelong source of comfort and self-soothing. I could only sleep in Ethan's bed, the bed we brought back from his apartment in La Crosse. I covered up with the quilt I had commissioned from a quilter who pieced together Ethan's soft T-shirts, his favorite Hollister plaid shirts, and even some back pockets from his well-worn jeans. I couldn't see, hear, or touch my son, but I drew great comfort from wrapping myself in this "memory quilt" made from his familiar clothes.

On the first Mother's Day after Ethan died, he communicated to my friend Lynn, who has known Ethan since he was born, that she must get up out of church—in the middle of the Mass, no less, go to a garden center, and buy his mom a pink—her favorite color—geranium as a gift from him for Mother's Day. Obeying, Lynn shocked her husband as she got up and left him sitting in the pew. She walked into my backyard that morning bearing a lushly blooming pink geranium basket.

Lynn told me, "I didn't think twice about leaving church to purchase this gift, because the directive from Ethan was so clear!"

I cried as I took the gift from Ethan, admiring the delicate hue of pink, and hugged my friend. I tried to cover up inside that I felt sad. Why didn't Ethan communicate directly with me? Was it because I was insensitive to him in the last conversation the day before he died? I had not felt him communicating to me personally since he died, though I desperately wanted him to. He had communicated to me through my friends and the medium…but not directly to me. What was I doing wrong? Was there something wrong with me?

I decided to meet with the medium a third time right after Mothers' Day, wanting to understand why Ethan was not communicating with me. I also hoped for forgiveness from Ethan for not being compassionate enough with him in our last conversation. As Stacey had instructed me in the past, I mediated prior to the session, calmed my heart and mind, and lovingly asked Ethan to be present at the meeting. As I sat down and told her what my questions were, she surprised me by first speaking directly to me as a psychic and said, "Robin, your throat chakra is blocked and congested with black, unexpressed, bottled up emotion. Ethan told you in our first meeting that you are shrouded in your grief like a grey mist. He says he is trying to guide you now, as you guided him when he was alive. But you still are shrouded. You must hear him when he tells you that you had no control to avert his death. It was not within your circle of influence to change the outcome of his life."

She instructed me to "stop being like a hamster on a wheel" and replaying over and over again that last conversation with Ethan. She asked me, "Have you given yourself permission to simply lose it, Robin? You are still so much in your head; you need to get into your feeling body. Please explore opportunities to focus on healing your grief, perhaps get away somewhere, heal your soul. Ethan does not blame you for anything. You have nothing for which to blame yourself. You need to let go of your judgement of yourself."

I was not able to heed this advice. I realized much later that it was because I would not be ready to let go of my judgment of myself for a long time.

One cold, damp, spring day after Ethan's birthday celebration, I was running around the indoor track at the Pettit Olympic Speed Skating Center. I was soothed as always by the repetition of my laps around the track, watching the speed skaters gliding swiftly past me on the ice rink inside the running track. The rink was chalky white ice, gouged by the skaters as they swung by in tight groups of waving arms and crouching bodies. Ice shards flew up from under their blades. As I rounded the curve of the track, I saw the Zamboni cross the running track and enter the rink to groom the ice. As the Zamboni circled the rink leaving smooth watery stripes behind it, the ice seemed to magically clear, the chalkiness softening into beautiful clear sparkling glass. I felt like the ruined ice—gouged, chipped, and broken—opaque and cold. I wanted to be made smooth and clear, and to be able to see through my opaqueness into my heart where I might find my son. But I was shrouded. I was lost even to myself.

Chapter 11
TOGETHER IN THE DEEP

In those first months of numbness and pain, I invited my husband to attend my grief counseling sessions with me because we were growing further apart. I knew from my training that strain in a marriage is very common after the death of a child, and that many couples separate and even divorce as a result of this strain. I also knew that it is normal that men and women grieve differently. Knowing this, however, did not seem to help me cope with my lived experience of the loneliness of our diverging grief journeys. My husband left the house three times and stayed elsewhere in those first awful nine months, as we tried, but were unable, to be of much comfort to each other. I was consumed with my searching for answers to my questions about Ethan's death, but he did not feel the same driving need to answer those questions. My searching took me down a long road away from Jeff.

At a session with our grief counselor, I learned that Jeff had turned to another woman for emotional support since Ethan died. I had no idea that this was occurring, which is probably evidence as to how disconnected we were from each other. I felt betrayed and angry, but gradually my anger faded, as I simply did not have the energy to fuel my anger. Grief overshadowed everything. I did not have the energy to ask him to leave, as I knew I could not function living alone. We refocused our grief therapy sessions toward repairing the broken trust between us.

Despite this wound to our marriage, we continued to plan our spring trip to Kauai with Deva, her husband, and his parents to celebrate their one year wedding anniversary. My daughter suggested we bring a vial of Ethan's ashes to spread somewhere on the island, so he also could be there as part of this celebration. My daughter was generous and wise to include Ethan. We decided toward the end of the trip to spread Ethan's ashes at the place where the Kilauea River meets the Pacific Ocean. The brackish ocean water swirls in and meets the fresh river water, mixing together harmoniously. In the Hawaiian tradition, we removed the plumeria blossoms from our leis and placed them in a pretty bowl. We sat on some warm flat rocks sheltered from the setting sun by a low tree hanging over the river.

As we placed each blossom in the water, floating them out to the ocean, Jeff suggested we each share a positive memory of Ethan:

"I remember how much you loved to play Uno and Trouble, and how much you loved to win!" I said.

Deva said, "I remember your amazing, intense hugs; you were the most genuine hugger of anyone I know, Ethan."

Jeff said, "Ethan, I loved watching you play the piano, singing along as you figured out songs by Ben Folds or Jack Johnson by just listening to them. It was heartwarming to see you so completely immersed in your love for music. In those moments, you were one with your music."

When all of the purple, pink, and red blossoms were floating, we divided the vial of ashes into our three cupped palms and gently tossed Ethan into the air. Bone and dust flew up, the bone settled down more quickly. The light, airy, dust sparkled as it sifted more slowly down through the rays of the setting sun. We watched a surprising amount of bone fragments settle into the shallow sandy river bottom, finally growing still. And there Ethan lay. One of us, probably his dad, joked that it would just figure that Ethan, being so big and tall, would have such heavy bone fragments that he could not be washed away by the river current! We laughed together, and then walked back to our rented house. We spent the evening as a group taking turns listening to songs that Ethan had learned on the piano and guitar and had sang for us so many times whenever he came home to visit. We felt sadness, but also some peace, as we celebrated with memories of Ethan that last night on the island of Kauai.

Two months into working on repairing our marriage, Jeff and I jumped off the bridge together over the outlet on Lake Noquebay. It was not what it sounds! Every summer for thirty years, my family had vacationed on this beautiful lake in northern Wisconsin. I don't recall us ever jumping off this bridge together. This is a tradition the locals in the Crivitz area engage in, almost like a rite of passage. The lake narrows at the outlet, and is funneled into a dam that propels the water strongly under the bridge and down the outlet on the other side. A deep bay of swirling water gathers after tumbling over the dam, perfect for jumping into for those who are brave and daring. For some reason, we decided to jump together that morning in July 2017, six months after Ethan died.

We stood on the bridge at the railing overlooking the outlet, smiling a bit as we remembered Ethan as a boy boasting about his jumping off the bridge, despite our admonishments as parents to both of our kids *not to jump off of the bridge*. Every parent there says that to their kids, and every kid seems to end up jumping anyway. We climbed up onto the wide steel railing and stood there pausing. A cloud passed over the sun, and the lake water lost its sparkle. It looked black and cold. I felt a chill. We held hands with the intention of jumping together, but I dropped off the railing a split second after he did, and we lost contact. Falling through the air took longer than

I expected. I couldn't tell if I was still chilled or not; I was only aware of falling. I held my nose to prevent the surge of lake water up my nostrils, but my hand flew off my face as my arm hit the water. The water felt so hard, the impact so much more violent than I expected. Dark murky water whooshed around my body, bubbling. I was plummeting fast. I couldn't feel my legs under me. I couldn't see or feel Jeff nearby. Where was he? I was straining to stop sinking into the deep. My freefall finally slowed, I found my legs, and I started to kick. My arms started to stroke. I needed to pull myself up to the surface where there was air and light. I needed to breathe.

My "other Robin" encouraged me, "Keep kicking, Robin, keep kicking through the black water toward the top where you can see light and sun. You can do it, Robin."

But it was so hard to stroke upward toward the light, because the strong current from the dam kept pushing me sideways and back down. I struggled against the current to get to the bank. I wasn't sure if I could get there alone. I finally saw Jeff swimming some distance away from me. I tried calling out to him, but my mouth got full of water. Scared, I just had to keep on swimming alone.

Experiencing the loss of our son as a couple has been similar to jumping off that bridge together. We tried to stay connected, but much of the time after Ethan died, we lost our connection in the midst of our grief. We lost connection in small ways, and in some very critical ways. Often, we were each alone, each trying to swim out of the black depths of our grief and get to where there was light to see our way, air to breathe, and hope with which to warm ourselves. When we had the energy or the desire to call out to the other with help or encouragement, we often did not hear the other, or sometimes our words simply fell flat and missed entering each other's hearts.

Jeff and I were broken as a couple from the trauma of trying to help Ethan even before his death. The eight years Ethan struggled with depression, anxiety, and substance abuse took a heavy toll on our marriage. Our marriage occupied an increasingly smaller part of our emotional and psychological space as our focus (particularly mine) became helping Ethan. Our conversations usually began like this: "Hi, how was your day? Have you heard from Ethan? How did he sound? What did he say?" We frequently never got past those details as they were often concerning, even frightening.

Ethan attempted suicide three times in those years. Two of those times we were frantically searching for him alongside a river. His dad found him alongside the Root River near our home just in time to be whisked away by ambulance and intubated in the nearest Emergency Department. Jeff told me that day, "My whole life I will *never* be able to un-see Ethan lying unconscious on the path next to the river." His comment unknowingly foreshadowed the traumatic grief that was building up inside of both of us. Two years later, after almost an hour of distraught searching, we found him weaving unsteadily along the Mississippi River. We led Ethan to a picnic table in the park alongside the river to figure out what to do next. I suddenly was suffused with anger and slapped him on his arms and shoulders as he crossed his arms on the rough table, hanging his head between them. I cried, "Ethan, what have you done? Why didn't you just call us, or someone else?" I suddenly stopped, sobbing, and lay my head on Ethan's shoulder. Jeff gently lifted me off of our son, and together we got him into our car and took him to the Emergency Department.

This grief lay buried, with no time or space to safely process it, because all of our emotional energy was directed toward coping with one crisis after another.

Ethan was living with us at age twenty-two, after being discharged from the hospital back to our care. One summer afternoon, he disappeared without telling us where he was going, despite his agreement to let us know if he needed to leave for *any reason* at all. After two hours of frantic searching, we were ready to call 911. Just then, Ethan rode up our driveway on his bike with a backpack on his back. He came inside, and we sat down at the dining room table asking for an explanation as to why he violated his safety plan with us. He explained that he had intended to stab himself after riding on the bike path near our house but changed his mind. He opened up his backpack and showed us the kitchen butcher knife he had placed inside. He said that after he pressed the tip of the blade against his chest, he decided to stop. We were shaken and so grateful he was able to stop himself. I put on my therapist hat as I had done so many times with him and asked questions like, "Why did you want to hurt yourself, Ethan? Did you use anything today? Did you want to die? How would killing yourself solve the issues you have? What caused you to change your mind? Will that be a reliable solution should you feel this way again? Will you reach out to someone if you feel like killing yourself? Who will you reach out to? How can you keep yourself safe? Do you need our help to stay safe? Please tell us how we can help you." This type of conversation is one I had many times with clients over the years, but it is scary to have this conversation with one's own child. I buried my mother's fear and tried to help him develop a plan that he could utilize. I told him he had to discuss his suicidal feelings with his doctor. He said to us, "I'm so sorry for worrying you guys."

These, and many other traumatic experiences of trying to help our son over the years, layered on top of one another inside of Jeff and I until we were overflowing with grief even before he died.

I recall a weekend trip during that first fall that I arranged for Jeff and I to get away to Madison to distract ourselves, and try to have a little fun. We booked a night in the renovated Edgewater Hotel near the Capitol, a beautiful example of art deco architecture. After a bike ride, we went to dinner at The Boathouse on the pier of Lake Mendota. It was a disaster. My husband chose that dinner to discuss a heavy topic, and it did not go well. We had a bitter argument. After dinner, he went back to the hotel, and I went for a walk alone. It was a warm night. Without a plan, I found myself walking toward the university, where college students thronged the sidewalks the closer I got to the shore of Lake Mendota. It became late, but I continued walking, feeling a sense of despair and deep loneliness. I walked to an area where many boats were slipped a distance out from the dock. I walked to the end of the dock, and looking out toward the boats, I saw a boat glowing with warm yellow light. For some reason, at that moment it seemed like the port I had been longing for...I imagined that the water was soft and warm like the night air, and that I could dive in and start swimming toward that cheerily lit boat. I wanted to be somewhere safe, feeling a respite from the discord between Jeff and me, from the pain of missing Ethan, from blaming myself for so much...I leaned forward, trembling, contemplating diving into the water. I heard footsteps behind me, and slightly turning, I saw a young couple step out onto the dock and then hesitate when they saw me. Suddenly, I saw myself as they must have seen me—a crazy person about to jump into a lake at midnight on a Saturday night! I straightened myself, turned, and walked past them off the dock. It took me an hour to walk back to the hotel. My fantasy that my husband would be waiting for me, wanting to make things right was just that: a fantasy. He was asleep. I curled up on the couch in our big expensive room and fitfully tried to rest.

Just as Ethan kept valiantly trying to get it right in his recovery, the next morning we woke up and tentatively tried to salvage the day. We went for a walk in the sunshine, felt soothed, and went to brunch. We chatted lightly, trying to stay away from anything difficult. I privately wondered how many more times we had it in us to keep trying to reconnect as a couple.

Chapter 12
TAKING ACTION

"Opioids, including prescription drugs and illicit versions
such as heroin and fentanyl, played a role in nearly
48,000 deaths in the U.S. in 2017-making them
the nation's leading cause of accidental deaths."
- The Centers for Disease Control and Prevention

As we approached nine months after Ethan's death, I had a recurring clear dream that fall. I dreamed that I was pregnant and in my third trimester. I attributed this dream to possibly yearning to have Ethan as my child back in my life, or maybe that I wanted another baby, as crazy as that seemed. When I shared this dream with Mary, a wise friend, she saw it instead as a sign that I was approaching the end of my quest of searching for answers, unearthing clues, and unraveling the reasons for Ethan's death. She saw it as a culmination of a long journey of searching that was coming finally to a birthing place within me. She saw it as birthing a new chapter in my life. I thought that I was indeed at the end of my searching. Some moments, I actually felt peace.

I prepared to take on a big promotion at work. I started facilitating a grief support group. I gave many community talks and presentations on the Opioid Epidemic.

I have always been a doer, though this had gone underground within me after Ethan died. However, nine months after his death, I felt a resurgence of energy rise up within me. I found in the next year that this energy was both a blessing and a curse. I found meaning in the activism I began engaging in, but it also took a toll on me that I was only to fully realize in the second year after Ethan's death. I began to take action against the Opioid Epidemic, the wave of drugs that killed my son. I had asked my best friend JeMae to give one of three eulogies that we planned for Ethan's funeral. She said these words, describing this epidemic, which I wasn't able to say in front of the hundreds of people at his funeral on January 3rd, 2017: "Ethan was one of ninety-one people who die every day from opiate addiction in our country. Until opiate addiction is fully acknowledged and treated as the illness that it is, those who are victimized by its addictive power will continue to suffer from limited treatment options, while living under the stigma of failure, shame, and hopelessness that makes full recovery much harder, relapse more likely, and life that much more painful."

I suggested we direct the money raised for Ethan's Fund toward supporting opiate addiction treatment at The Dewey Center in Wauwatosa, Wisconsin, one of the places where Ethan had received excellent treatment. My husband agreed. We felt sure that Ethan would have wanted those monetary gifts to go toward helping others in their fight against opiate addiction. Ethan's Fund provided the impetus for me and my husband to agree to be interviewed by the philanthropy department of my employer. We described the story of Ethan's life and his long struggle with depression and addiction. As the first anniversary of his death approached, and with our permission, this interview—broken down into six different chapters—was disseminated via email to thousands of people along with an invitation to give to Ethan's Fund. The last chapter of his story was sent out just prior to the one year anniversary of his death. This was an effective way to inspire people to donate to Ethan's Fund.

Even though I had given permission, this fundraising campaign took an emotional toll on me. I was in a visible leadership role within my organization. I was often blindsided in large meetings with mention made of this campaign, whether it was a report about the progress of the campaign, or myself being asked a question about Ethan's Fund, or opening my email to read a mass email sent to employees encouraging them to donate to this Fund, or the most difficult—a large photo of my family being splashed up on a screen in a conference room without my prior knowledge. The photo displayed was of our intact family at Christmas in 2014, just two weeks after Ethan graduated from college. Ethan, his older sister Deva, his dad, and myself are laughing and holding hands. The joy on our faces is wonderful, and I am so grateful for that moment being captured forever. But that photo becoming so public when my grief was still so fresh often stopped my breath. It knocked me off of my carefully protected persona that I slipped into each day as I arrived at work. I quickly learned that the only way I could survive in my role was to bury my emotional pain, trying to safeguard my composure at work. I distanced myself more and more from my vulnerability, trying to be brave, for the sake of "Ethan's Story" and the power it had to raise money for Ethan's Fund.

Area media sources, too, picked up on Ethan's story as the opiate crisis was pronounced to be an "epidemic" by President Trump, and subsequently declared to be a "National Emergency." I spoke about Ethan's story on local TV stations. I was well aware that part of the interest in Ethan's story was that his mother was a licensed psychotherapist and substance abuse counselor of almost thirty years, his father a police detective, and his sister also a psychotherapist. If our family could lose a loved one to drug overdose, it made the point without saying that no family, no one, no socioeconomic group, was exempt from this epidemic.

One TV reporter and her photographer came into our home for an interview. They photographed the large cedar chest that was covered with mementos I had placed there after Ethan's funeral almost a year earlier: his college diploma, his cap tassel he had hung on his rearview mirror, his glasses, his guitar capo, a smiling photo of him and his girlfriend. There was also a photo of him with his middle school basketball team looking proud and so serious on one bent knee in the front row, his high school graduation picture, his sobriety coin from one of his treatment stays. There was the framed cross stitch piece made by my sister Renee commemorating Ethan's birth on March 6th, 1991, saying, "In like a lion, out like a lamb." His darling baby shoes, his wallet, and his Lakers lanyard, all interlaced with a string of white lights that I kept lit all the time. I couldn't put these tangible signs of his life away after the funeral, so there they were, almost a year later. For that interview, I wore a black T-shirt with the words "Never Give Up" in white letters on it. I would have continued to fight with Ethan to help him find his way to health until I was eighty, ninety, one hundred.

Now, I was going to do whatever I could, with what was left of my reservoir of energy God had gifted to me, to help area communities respond to the scourge of this crisis as it killed loved ones in their midst. I knew deep within me that I was born to be a healer and a teacher. I started to feel on fire. I spoke publicly in the community at health fairs, symposiums, and coalitions as we approached and passed the one year anniversary of Ethan's death. As I saw Ethan's Fund growing to over $46,000 by the end of 2017, I felt deep gratitude welling up within me that was inspired by the generosity of so many givers to this fund. If I couldn't save Ethan, perhaps I could be an instrument to help save someone else from the horrors of opiate addiction. This gratitude at times softened my grief.

I wanted to help educate young people about addiction. I spoke at area high school health classes on drug addiction, and the students were surprised at the bleak description I painted of the life of someone addicted to opiates. Opiate addiction is a terrible vise upon one's body, mind, and spirit. It narrows the user's daily life to a one-dimensional need for the drug to even feel normal. They seemed to think that the life of a drug user was like a party all the time. Nothing could be further from the truth. Intense cravings for opiates can very quickly take over the brain, because our brain is wired via opiate receptors to seek pleasure. Once these receptors experience the effects of an opiate—whether prescription painkillers, heroin, fentanyl, or morphine—abuse can occur quickly, causing an escalating need for more opiates as tolerance for the ingested amount increases. I told the students that opioid use—even short term—can lead to addiction and too often, overdose.

I expanded my efforts and decided to also reach out to help the other victims of this epidemic—the left behind parents, siblings, and spouses. I felt that I was making a difference. I would realize much later that my activism was also born of a subconscious need to distract myself from the unrelenting pain of the loss of my son, and the shame I carried with me of not being able to keep him alive. Burying my grief in helping others heal would eventually be part of my own undoing.

Chapter 13
THE MUSTARD SEED

There is a story of a woman who came to the Buddha seeking help after the death of her child. She was told that in order to be healed she only needed to find a mustard seed from a household that had never known loss. According to the story, she traveled far and wide in vain, never finding such a household, but instead she found riches like understanding, compassion, friendship, and truth. I felt that one way for me to learn how to live each day with the reality of Ethan being gone forever was to be amongst others who had suffered this same catastrophic loss. I needed to burrow into every corner of my loss and try to understand how to cope, how to heal. I had been reading everything I could on grief, but I needed to also talk with others. I rely on verbal processing. My husband was not able to meet my huge need to process and talk through my grief. My best self accepted the differences in our grief journey. My worst self resented these differences.

I decided to try attending a nationally based grief support group for family members who have lost a loved one to addiction called GRASP (Grief Recovery After Substance Passing). I did, indeed, find compassion and understanding and friendship through GRASP over time. However, the first time I attended a meeting, just weeks after Ethan died, I was completely overwhelmed. As I stood and abruptly walked out as the meeting drew to a close, another mother named Jodi came hurrying after me.

She reached out to me saying, "I know this is hard for you, it is so recent that you lost your son, but I'm glad you came. The reason we are all here really sucks, doesn't it? But we help each other figure out how to make it through a day. Please come back!"

Standing there in the doorway, she gave me a soft pat on the shoulder, and then seeing my crumpling face, gave me a hug. It was her warm, friendly touch that motivated me to attend again, because I honestly had no memory of what was said in that first meeting. I attended several more times during those first nine months; once my daughter came with me. It was draining for me to attend regularly due to the long forty-minute drive one way, particularly in Midwest winter weather. Grieving people need help and resources that don't take much energy to access, given that sometimes making it through one minute to the next can be overwhelmingly hard.

In 2016, there were 827 opioid deaths due to overdose in Wisconsin (Wisconsin Department of Health Services) and yet there were only two GRASP chapters in all of the state. Where were all of those parents, spouses, and adult siblings getting their support for this type of loss that has so much stigma and shame associated with it? I decided to start my own GRASP chapter in my community of Greenfield, located in Milwaukee County. I applied for permission to become a facilitator through the organization. GRASP was started in 2002 by a couple who lost their daughter to drug overdose. They require that facilitators have the lived experience of a loss of a child, and that they typically wait at least a year or more before starting their own chapter. I convinced myself that due to my training, I was emotionally able and prepared to start my own chapter at nine months after Ethan died.

An unexpected blessing was my husband's willingness to attend and support me in building this group. As a retired police officer, he set a positive example for the men attending the group that a man could feel safe expressing his grief in a group setting, or to attend and simply listen. Gradually, more women brought their husbands, partners, and brothers. Jeff warmly welcomed these men. Our Greenfield GRASP group has had quite a number of couples who are also struggling with how to support each other when they are drowning in their own sea of grief. Liz, a strong and smart mother in our group, lost her son at age twenty-one to a drug overdose. She and her husband are still parenting two teenage daughters, and she has shared with our group her view that, "Recovering as a family from such a loss is like trying to throw out life preservers to each other when you are drowning yourself."

The individuals, couples, and families that attend our GRASP group all have their own stories in their journeys of trying to help their loved one survive drug addiction. They come to GRASP to survive the common experience of being completely overwhelmed in the traumatic aftermath of their loved one succumbing to the disease of addiction. Bearing witness to a story of loss whenever a new person joins the group is heartbreaking and even somewhat re-traumatizing. But it is a price we are willing to bear, because without holding each other's hands, some of us don't know how we would keep standing.

Erin, a member of our group who lost her brother to a drug overdose, has excellent powers of observation, a kind heart, and a healing manner about her. She also cuts to the chase—in short, she is a nurse. During a meeting about a year after our group's formation, she said in front of the entire group, "Robin, you don't need to hold it all together so much. This group is for you, too." Surprised, and caught off guard that she had called me out, albeit lovingly, I felt myself starting to emotionally give way a tiny bit. I was exhausted. I was working long work days after my promotion into a new leadership role. After work, I was either going to a strength training class, teaching or attending yoga classes, attending community meetings, or chairing my church board meetings. I routinely got home after 8:30 p.m. every night. I was staying as busy as I could, I realize now looking back, in order to stave off the cascade of grief that always seemed to threaten to overtake me. I refused to give in to the seduction of allowing myself to emotionally sink into my pain. I kept compartmentalizing it and kept on advocating, speaking out, helping others, and raising money for Ethan's Fund.

Chapter 14
EMOTIONAL ICU

During the first year of my grief journey, I had a recurring nightmare, and it was the same every time. I am standing alone on the front lawn of our first home on the east end of Greenfield. This is where Jeff and I started and then nurtured our new family. We lived there until Ethan was six and Deva was eight years old. As I am standing under the enormous silver maple tree shading the front of the house, I begin to hear a cracking and snapping. I gasp, thinking, "That huge tree is going to fall on our house!" But as I look up, I see that what is snapping is the roof shingles. They start to snap off one by one as the roof cracks in several places and begins to slowly fold in on itself. I stand there, aghast, as I watch in horror. There is no debris from the roof falling down around me, because it caves in. Strangely, it falls without much of a sound. No one is noticing but me. There is no help rushing in. The roof seems to take forever to fall, and I cannot move as I watch, mesmerized. I am helpless to do anything but watch, watch as the house where my children were babies—where we had such bright hope and joy as new parents—is crushed by the crumpling roof that had sheltered the young family who had blossomed beneath it.

"It's odd that you can get so absorbed by your own pain
or your own problem that you don't quite fully share
the hell of someone close to you."
– Lady Bird Johnson

Living with one's spouse from whom you are estranged is the
loneliest way to live. Jeff and I were trying to salvage our marriage, but
we barely had enough emotional energy to try to cope with our grief,
much less rebuild a marriage. Jeff described to me what he wanted
one day toward the end of the first year: "All I want to do is go live
in a hotel room somewhere warm and sunny and hang my laundry
on the balcony railing to dry. I don't want any responsibilities, any
problems to solve, and no one that I have to take care of or protect."

I had no idea how to respond to his feelings. They were in such
contrast to how I was coping by working more hours, doing advo-
cacy activities, providing educational presentations, and facilitating
a grief group. His wanting to go live in a hotel room felt like abandonment of me. I was angry at him and hurt.

It was two years later, when Jeff was learning to share more of
his feelings of grief, that he wrote these words in a note to me: *Being
in law enforcement doesn't exactly encourage honest expression of emotions. To do so may actually be counterproductive to staying safe in high
risk situations. But, managing stress by burying feelings doesn't work so
well in one's personal life. I know my unexpressed emotions manifested
themselves at times in anger and frustration. As a cop, I was trained to
'protect and serve.' For me, my inability to protect Ethan from his addiction crumbled the very foundation on which my career as a cop was built.*

Without that insight from him at that time to explain his desire
to flee to a hotel room, I distanced myself from him and further immersed myself into my work and activities. The sharp differences in
how we were coping in our grief caused the rift between us to keep
widening. We struggled to meet each other halfway. We each were
yearning for relief from the pain of learning to live life in this new
reality that would never change—the reality that our son was dead.

What I most longed for was a soft voice, a kind hand patting
me, soothing me, murmuring that it will be okay, that I will survive,

I can get through this. I wanted someone to hold my hand and shepherd me through this searing desert of loss. I wanted someone with whom I could completely fall apart. My husband was not that person. He was trying to stay afloat himself. He told me that he thought I had a "personality disorder" when I allowed myself to express my intense grief in the privacy of our home. My behavior was actually likely the early signs of Post-Traumatic Stress Disorder showing itself within me. I ignored the signs.

I found myself starting to rely more and more on my adult daughter. I regret now putting her in that position. Deva is a deeply caring and reliable woman who has a steely steadiness about her. I suspect she covered up her own grief at times when she worried about me, and her father, too. Trauma has a way of dividing people, especially families, leading to fragmenting of relationships already splintered by the traumatic loss. So, we asked her to see our grief counselor with us as a family. The three of us were thankfully able to have some healing conversations in that counselor's office. I was able to hear from Deva that the intensity of my grief as a mother losing a son sometimes overshadowed her grief as a sister losing a brother. The counselor stressed that Deva's "experience of losing a brother is different, but no less important, than that of a parent losing a child." The counselor normalized the stress in our marriage which was so evident to Deva. We wanted her to know that we were fighting to keep our family whole. Those gentle sessions helped me feel that our family was united in our efforts to grieve the loss of Ethan, but also to try to recall happier times with him. Frankly, that was hard, as the last several years of his life were so stressful.

I painfully learned that in our circle of friends there were those who could not walk this walk with me and left our friendship. Yet, I also experienced the surprising gift of others stepping into this grief journey with me with their whole heart. But friends have to go home at some point, and live their own lives. I begged God to give me the strength to endure the pain of this journey. I got angry again at God. I told him, "I need someone right here, someone I can see and touch, someone who will pick me up when I fall, who will help me keep going when I wake up every morning with the reality that my son is dead, biting cruelly down on my shoulders like a heavy iron yoke." Who is that person and where are they?

My journal entries in the second year after Ethan's death revealed the growing cracks in my ability to function. I wrote about struggling more often with being in large groups, around loud noises, or when too many things were going on at the same time. I began to feel inexplicably fearful. Previously simple decisions such as what to wear or how to plan my day became more complicated and required extra energy on my part to execute. I fell twice in one week because I sometimes felt unsure of where my feet were landing under me.

One day, as I was driving to meet Jeff for lunch, a car hit my right front quarter panel and sped off. Stunned, I pulled over to the side of the road. I couldn't think straight. I decided to keep driving to the restaurant. I parked, and we had lunch. When we walked out to the parking lot, he gasped, and said, "What happened to the car?" I said, "I think a car hit me on my way here." It apparently didn't register with me as being the significant event that it was. I didn't care. I felt so wounded and so sad. Jeff and I circled around one another. Jeff would get angry at me, telling me that I was acting "crazy." I did feel crazy sometimes.

I began to dread going to sleep because I feared having this recurring nightmare: I am driving on an asphalt road that keeps crumbling at the edges into the roiling brownish water surging up on either side of the ribbon of road I am traveling on. I find myself looking down upon my car with me inside, watching myself driving faster and faster to keep ahead of the road disintegrating right from underneath me.

In my journal, I describe a night when I was desperate for help:

Last night after I got home from yoga at 8:30pm, I showered, and then tried to read, but I couldn't concentrate. My heart started hammering, my throat hurt and ached with tears...at 9:30pm I got up off of the couch, packed a bag, and drove to a hospital about five miles from our house. It was coincidentally the hospital where Ethan was born. I parked in the parking lot next to the front entrance and looked up at all of the glowing lit rooms. I so wanted to be in one of those rooms, lying in one of those safe beds, being taken care of by someone whose job it was to take care of my wounded-ness, to minister to me, to smooth my brow, to help me feel safe, to heal my sorrow...I sat in my dark car with the heater on high because it was below zero outside. What exactly would I say if I walked into that hospital? "Please, can I have a room here? I need one of those rooms with the soft lights and someone coming in during the night to check in on me. Please help me because my heart is so broken, and I just can't keep it together anymore."

I didn't walk into the hospital, and I didn't say those words to anyone. I kept looking up at those warm glowing windows, the rectangle shapes blurred by my tears until they seemed like sparkling points of lights against a black background. I prayed out loud to God, "What should I do? Where can I go?" I even prayed out loud to Ethan to please help me. I said out loud, "Robin, now you are for sure getting mixed up praying to Ethan..." I continued to sit there in the car. I breathed in and out, over and over again, as I do in a yoga class. Finally calmer, I drove home. It was after midnight.

There were many moments like these of utter desperation that ground me to a halt, feeling broken, wondering how this was ever going to get better.

In the GRASP meetings I facilitate, we have discussed many times the importance of acknowledging our traumatic loss as an emotional wound of such magnitude that if it were a physical wound, we would likely need to be in an Intensive Care Unit. But where is the ICU for wounds of grief? What would such a place look like? Who would care for us if we were to come and stay there, trying to repair our lives broken from years of living, loving, or caring for an addicted loved one? Who are these caregivers who would want to work at such a place? Where would we find them?

They are us. *We* must provide this tender care for ourselves and for each other. As the opiate epidemic continues to wreak devastation across the United States, thousands of parents, families, and spouses are in desperate need of a soft, safe place to go to heal when healing seems impossible.

My grief counselor shared with me a poem written by Hafiz, a Persian poet who lived and wrote in the 1300s. He understood even then the concept of an emotional ICU in his poem, "A Cushion For Your Head."

Just sit there right now.
Don't do a thing.
Just rest.
For your separation from God,
From love,
Is the hardest work in this world.

Let me make you trays of food
and something that you like to drink.
You can use my soft words
As a cushion for your head.

(*The Gift*, translated by Daniel Ladinsky, 1999, Penguin Compass)

Chapter 15
ON MY YOGA MAT

My yoga practice was possibly the single most healing thing for me to do in managing my grief, prior to starting my brain-spotting work with a trauma therapist eighteen months after Ethan died. In fact, I took my very first yoga class in 2008, when Ethan became ill, because I needed something to help me cope with the trauma of his first suicide attempt. Both yoga and brain-spotting have in common a key quality in that they are a body-centered and mindfulness-based modality. Yoga helps me to get out of my head and into my body and just *be* me in the moment—letting go of all of my roles and expectations of myself. When I unroll my mat and begin to practice, I feel calm spreading throughout my body as my nervous system is soothed by the breath and body work that are the hallmarks of a hatha yoga class. Deepening my yoga practice by studying to be a yoga teacher during the years that Ethan's addiction worsened, helped me to keep grounded in being *myself* separate from being the mother of an ill son.

When I am practicing yoga, I am able to access my spiritual self. In fact, all my life, it has been when moving my physical body that I am most able to connect with God. I often talk to God, and I listen to what God has to say to me, when I am running, walking, kayaking, swimming, or hiking—any silent sport, preferably in nature, can be a spiritual experience for me. My yoga practice has helped me cope with some of my most difficult life experiences.

Being guided by Gina, my nephew Joel's fiancé and a compassionate yoga teacher, through a yoga practice early in the morning of Ethan's funeral helped me make it through that wrenching experience. Through her, God held out His hand to me on my mat and gave me the strength to get up and honor Ethan.

Eleven months later, it was in that same yoga studio on a late Friday afternoon that I finally perceived Ethan. I was alone in the softly lit studio after a long work week, practicing my sequencing to teach my 5:30 pm "Happy Hour" yoga class. I finished preparing and simply sat down on my mat, breathing and stilling myself into a meditative place. I found it hard to meditate after Ethan died, due to the traumatic memories that typically swarmed into my head. On that afternoon, for some reason I was in a very peaceful place within myself.

After some time, from the left side of my body a few feet away, I strongly sensed someone—or something. I opened my eyes and turned toward it. I saw—felt, actually, *with my body*, the shape of a presence, of something next to me, quiet and calm. Then it was gone. It was pure energy—silvery, bright and pulsing.

Without even being aware of the words coming out of my mouth, I matter-of-factly said, "Hi Ethan, how are you, honey?" I startled myself, hearing my voice greeting him! I stood up on my mat and looked around the studio. I started to feel sad; it seemed that I had spoken to the air. The longer I stood still, the more I felt unsure of what might have just happened. I told myself, "It might not have been Ethan, but take some comfort in *believing* that was him, Robin. Ethan would want that for you."

Just to make sure I got his message, Ethan communicated to me again two days later. Jeff and I decided to buy a live Christmas tree for the first time in over twenty years. We decided to put purple and gold lights on it in honor of Ethan's favorite basketball team, the

Lakers. One idea led to another, and we hung ornaments that he had made as a child on its fragrant branches. Then we hung his baby shoes, his red toddler winter hat, his college graduation cap tassel, framed photos of him smiling—anything of his that would hang on a tree, we hung. When we finished, we stepped back and knew that Ethan would have been delighted to come home for Christmas to that tree—he loved having the spotlight shone on him!

That night, I had a dream that Ethan was laughing and teasing me and saying, "Geez, mom, it took me dying to have you and Dad decorate the Christmas tree just all about me?! I love it! Thanks!" That is exactly the kind of snarky thing Ethan would have said. Perhaps it truly was him appearing to me in my dream. I wanted to believe so.

Chapter 16
OPIOID CRISIS CONGRESS

After that first Christmas after Ethan's death, I read a news story about the pharmaceutical giant, Purdue Pharma, deciding to stop marketing OxyContin, widely referred to in the media as its "pills of death," to medical doctors in light of the opioid crisis. Too late, I thought, to have saved Ethan or the thousands of others dying from opioid addiction. It was an empty gesture on their part, anyway, as medical providers already know about OxyContin, one of the most infamous prescription drugs on the market. A real gesture would have been to stop *making* the "pills of death." Wanting to learn more about this epidemic on the national level, I decided to attend the inaugural National Opioid Crisis Congress, February 2018, in Orlando, Florida. This coming together of policy makers, treatment providers, and law enforcement personnel from many states across the country was the first of its kind. The sharing of strategies, ideas, and programming was inspired by the states' realization that if the tragically spreading opioid crisis was going to turn around, change was going to need to happen at the community and state level.

As I listened and learned, I thought about a point Caroline Myss, PhD, made in her book, *Anatomy of a Spirit*, that, "Epidemics are a negative group experience to which we can become energetically susceptible, if our own personal first chakra fears and attitudes are similar to those held by the culture's overall first chakra orientation." The chakra system is a way of understanding seven energy centers which are housed within our physical body. The first chakra is our root chakra. It's our energetic ability to be grounded, stable, and safe in a foundation within ourselves and our lives, especially when under duress.

Dr. Myss's view of how disease can spread across a whole culture deeply resonated with me. As a psychotherapist, I have long observed that our cultural propensity to cover up emotional and physical discomfort, our desire to escape pain, or numb ourselves from it, puts us at a great risk for addiction to bloom. This risk increases when our inability to be grounded and stay present in the midst of our pain intersects with the highly addictive and lethal quality of opiates flowing out from our doctors', dentists', and psychiatrists' offices.

I stood up early in the first day of the conference when comments were invited and took a risk by introducing myself and saying, "I am a behavioral health therapist and substance abuse counselor and I am the mother of a son who died from a heroin overdose a year ago. I feel that our culture's abhorrence of pain, and often refusal to learn to tolerate pain—much less embrace it for what it can teach us—has put our country at a terrible crossroads. Readily available opiates, combined with our country's insatiable desire for narcotics to avoid pain of all kinds, have caused a conflagration burning through communities all around our country. While the opioid crisis was seeded due to physicians' prescribing opiates under the misinformation that they were not addictive, these seeds have bloomed into an epidemic because we demand immediate relief from pain! Our crossroads challenge is not *only* to help heal those suffering from this horrible addiction, but also as a culture to move *off* of a path wanting to disconnect from pain. We need to move *toward* a path of moving *through* and *coping* with pain—both physical and emotional—in more healthy ways." I sat down, surprised I had said so much.

Throughout the two-day conference, people came up to me and said, "You are the 'crossroads' lady; thank you for your comments!" and introduced themselves to me, wanting to engage with me in conversation, wanting to hear more of my ideas. I conversed with many attendees about the costs we pay as a society to avoid pain, both physical and emotional, through our use of substances as well as engaging in other pain-numbing behaviors. Also during the conference, I was interfacing with a reporter back in Milwaukee who was preparing a spot on the evening news about Ethan's story. I became overwhelmed by the intensity of everything I was professionally and personally experiencing there, but I pressed through it, and as always, I made it work. Attending this conference had an unexpected impact on me. It was a profound visual and experiential reminder that my family's loss of Ethan to this epidemic was replicated by thousands and thousands of families all over the country. I felt an enormous sense of solidarity with these families and a renewed commitment that I would do whatever I could to help families recover.

Chapter 17
CELEBRATING ETHAN

When I returned from the conference, Jeff surprised me over a Valentine's dinner at a favorite restaurant of ours, just two weeks away from Ethan's birthday, with a beautiful silver heart-shaped necklace. It was set with a blue aquamarine, Ethan's birthstone. He clasped it around my neck, and at that very moment, "Hey, Soul Sister" by Train played over the radio. Our family heard this song every morning whenever Ethan was home because it was his alarm in the morning. He would hit the snooze button repeatedly, so we heard the first few lines of that song over and over again. Smiling, we became still and listened, taken back to those years of trust and ease in our relationship with our son, when our family connected with each other—happy, and most wonderfully, all healthy. Ethan's spirit reached out to us on that Valentine's Day. It was as though he was prompting us to embrace this moment to celebrate and share happy memories of him, rather than letting grief take over all of our interactions together.

Over dinner, I said to Jeff, "Ethan's 27th birthday is 3 weeks away—let's plan a celebration of Ethan's life!"

I wanted to do for Ethan what we had done as a gift for our daughter on her college graduation day. We took her on a tour of all of the places in Milwaukee County that marked milestones in her life, starting from when she was born. Her dad wrote the itinerary in rhyming verses, and it was funny, sweet, and touching. Since Ethan's addiction had worsened after his college graduation, we never had a chance to do a "Milestone Tour" for him before he died. So, we planned out the route, and Jeff wrote the itinerary in verse. We all piled into our suburban with our best friends, their teenage daughter, as well as our daughter and her husband Jordan, and off we went on a tour of Ethan's life. Jeff wrote these verses to illuminate Ethan's life:

West Allis Memorial Hospital:
It all started here for me
And our family often said
That all the nurses on the ward
Remarked that I was born with such a big head!

Little Learner's Preschool:
Transitions were hard for me no matter the size
And this was no exception to the rule
So, it took me some time to adjust and adapt
The first time that I went to this school.

My First House:
I was here as a boy with a park across the street
With hardly a worry or care
Except every summer I wished Mom and Dad
Would have installed central air!

Piano Lessons with Mrs. Schultz:
Here I learned to tickle the ivories
With the utmost skill and all my might
If only the world would have been so simple
To always have been black and white.

Whitnall Middle School:
In this school I was always involved
In many different groups
But if I had to select a favorite one
It would be the one where I dunked on the hoops.

The Zelazo Center:
I often marched to a drummer's different beat
Keeping time with my feet and my hands
So, it wasn't too surprising to me
That I became the youngest member of the UW—M jazz band.

Ann's Pizza:
My first job was here for awhile
But I quit because I thought it wasn't fair
That every time I worked my shift
I had to climb a million stairs.

Whitnall High School:
Here I folded my gift for piano into my gift for guitar
I found "The Remedy" to soothe my soul
And for a very long time
Music helped to keep me whole.

Greenfield Department of Public Works:
I worked here during summers outside in the sun
Uncaring that my nose would blister
Every morning I woke up in my bed
To hear the tune of "Hey Soul Sister."

The King and I Thai restaurant:
Often I was too big for my britches
'Cuz I thought that I knew a lot
But I should have listened to the waiter
When he warned me that the food was really hot!

We all laughed and cried, too, as Jeff read his funny verses describing each stop along the journey of Ethan's life. These moments of humor and grace softened the hurtful impact of our emotional blunders with each other.

Life wasn't pausing for any of us to figure out how to grieve gracefully. Life didn't allow for any of us to step away in a big time-out until we were healed enough to carry on. Deva and Jordan were trying to build their new marriage, having married only six months before she lost her only sibling. Deva was growing her new career as an outpatient psychotherapist. Jeff was also trying, post-retirement, to develop a new career in International Risk Mitigation, which took him out of the country for periods of time. I was learning the ropes of my new role as a Director in Behavioral Health Services, teaching yoga, leading my church Board of Directors, and speaking and volunteering in the community. Our lives were very full. The work that grief demands saps one's strength to move forward. Sometimes all one can do is try to stay firmly planted, and not get swept overboard.

We planted ourselves with planning a huge event I called "Ethan's Run Against Addiction." I had been awakened suddenly in the middle of night on the first anniversary of Ethan's death with the unequivocal sense that I was receiving a message from Ethan.

He said, "Mom! Mom!" He often said my name twice when he

was excited or serious about something. "You've got to organize a race about my fight against my addiction. It will help other people!"

We are all runners in our family, so this was a perfect way to honor Ethan's fight. My husband and I were able to connect with each other around planning this event, as we worked closely with a committee of Greenfield City departments to host this event in beautiful Konkel Park in Greenfield. The Mayor as well as the Greenfield Police, Fire, Health, Parks and Recreation, and Public Works departments all generously contributed to making this race a reality. Rich Dodd, Ethan and Deva's former high school cross country coach, who is on his own journey of recovery, volunteered to be our Race Director. Ethan's godfather, Jon, gave his services to time the event for free. Ethan's girlfriend, Ariana, and her mother came from Minnesota, his roommates came from La Crosse, his uncle came from Phoenix, and many others came from all over Wisconsin to support this event. June 9th, 2018 dawned, and 764 runners and walkers left the starting line! Through this event, we were able to raise over $40,000 for Ethan's Fund to support opiate recovery treatment in the Milwaukee

area communities. We were so amazed by and grateful for the hundreds who came out for this event.

I was aware how much I was trembling, with a mixture of grief that we were even holding this event and joy that we actually pulled it off, as I prepared to give my remarks at the start of the race. I tried to quell my conflicting emotions. I stood near the top of a stepladder at the starting line and spoke out strongly into my microphone to the participants with these words: "We created this event for two reasons: we need to generate more acceptance for people with the disease of addiction—let's not call them addicts. That is a label, and it does not define who they are—and we need to eradicate the stigma associated with addiction. Stigma means marked by disgrace. Our loved ones deserve to be freed from the shame and disgrace that marks having the disease of addiction."

"So, with every step we take this morning, let's send this message to the world. Let's step with acceptance, and LOVE for those struggling with addiction. Step with openness and pride if you are in recovery or supporting someone in recovery."

"When Ethan was a little boy, he loved to proudly present me with a bouquet of dandelions he had picked, and he especially loved the ones going to seed because he would blow the seeds in my face and giggle mischievously at me. Let's all be like dandelion seeds and spread this message of love and acceptance out into the world!"

So many of us felt Ethan's presence that wonderful Saturday morning. It felt like a victory over his death—a victory full of celebration.

Ethan reaching out to us during our Valentine's dinner, after our Christmas tree decorating, and on my yoga mat, was so precious to me. I documented these interactions in my journal and reviewed them over and over again. I asked myself, could this really be my son reaching out to me, to us? Or were these coincidences? Where exactly *was* Ethan? What did it look like? What was he *doing*? How did he know when to reach out to us? How did he know what to do to get our attention?

Chapter 18
AFTERLIFE

"My Father's house has rooms to spare. If that weren't the case, would I
have told you that I am going to prepare a place for you?"
— John 14:2

We chose this as the verse for the cover of Ethan's funeral bulletin because Ethan felt so cared for when we prepared his boyhood
room for him whenever he came home to visit. It comforted us to
know that God loved Ethan and prepared a room for him in the
afterlife.

After sharing my questions with my women's group, Radhe
wanted me to read a book on near-death experiences. She had read
deeply into this genre and told me, "I think this may help you to
trust that Ethan is somewhere safe and that he is happy." I hesitat-
ed, saying, "I seem able only to read books on grieving, I don't think
I could read this." Radhe responded, "Take it and read it when you
feel ready."

Shortly after that, I was in an airport during a layover on my
way to the "Helping Parents Heal" conference in Scottsdale, Ari-
zona. This is a national organization that provides help and support to parents who have lost a child by any means. I impulsively
pulled Radhe's book out of my backpack and began reading *Proof
of Heaven*. To my wonderment, I encountered amazing stories of
descriptions of Heaven, or the afterlife, from people who had got-

ten close to Heaven, but because it wasn't their time to cross over, returned back to their physical bodies and their lives on this earth. Their similar reports of the peace and love they felt infusing their spirits while they were visiting the afterlife were a balm to my heart. Their experiences gave me a sense of hope. If my son was in the same place they visited before returning to their physical body, then he seemed to be in a place free of shame, illness, and pain! I felt such relief for Ethan as I read these stories that I cried in the airport lounge.

Contemplating Ethan being forever free of the cravings for opiates that tormented his mind and body and being free of the shame of the boundary crossings of his soul that he committed to satisfy those cravings, was a whole new way of thinking about Ethan for me. The torment one experiences while being in active addiction can be unrelenting in the toll it exacts on one's mind, body, and soul. My brother, Rolf, honored Ethan in the eulogy he shared at Ethan's funeral when he described the tremendous courage and the mighty effort it cost Ethan each day "to pick up his sword and shield and keep battling his addiction." Rolf spoke about the "demons" we all privately battle with inside of ourselves and can keep hidden from others, but the demon of addiction is blatantly visible to all who know someone in the vise of that demon. Ethan's three relapses in the last ninety days of his life must have cost him such shame, pain, and fear. In Heaven, Ethan was freed from all of that pain!

I felt like rejoicing. But my rejoicing was tinged with shame that I needed these stories in order to believe in the afterlife of Heaven. I was raised as a Christian to believe in Heaven as the place we go to be reunited with God and those that died before us. Faith is believing in that which we cannot see. My faith had been weakened and sapped by the pain of not getting any answers from God as to why Ethan died. I prayed for forgiveness from God for my weak faith. I thanked God for sending people back from Heaven who, after glimpsing its glory, could tell the rest of us here about what wonders await us there. God must know that many of us need that reassurance.

My husband shared my gladness for Ethan when I told him about the descriptions of Heaven—the afterlife that Ethan was now enjoying in a place of peace and love and light and freedom from pain. Jeff said, "I'm glad, too, for Ethan." Then he said angrily, "But what about those of us whom he left behind who are still full of pain and grief?" I was not able to meet Jeff in his place of anger. I had already worked so hard to move away from feeling angry at Ethan. Connecting with anger again could kill my fledgling sense of peace about where Ethan was now.

One morning, I woke up knowing that I was supposed to get a tattoo. I laughed and asked myself where in the world did that come from? I am so not a tattoo type of person. Another message from Ethan perhaps? When posing for photos with others, Ethan would always sling his left arm easily over the shoulder of whomever he was standing next to, because he was taller than just about anyone. Since Ethan went to be with God, I often prayed to God, who is taller and mightier than everyone: "God, Ethan is your son now—actually, sorry, You know he has always been your son, I had him for such a little while—please God, sling your arm around my dear son's shoulder, squeeze him, and give him a kiss on his cheek for me until I am with him in Heaven to do it myself." And so my tattoo on my right forearm says exactly that. A heart surrounds the words "Ethan 12-27-16…until I am with you in Heaven."

Attending the "Helping Parents Heal" conference exposed me

to new concepts about the afterlife I had never considered. I had recently read everything I could about George Anderson, a famous medium who specializes in communicating with deceased children's spirits. I learned that he would be there in-person, and I wanted to witness his readings. It was truly amazing to see him communicate with spirits wanting to connect with their parents in an audience of hundreds of grieving parents. I recall one young woman's spirit apologized to her mother in the audience for committing suicide at age twenty-one. She wanted her mother to know that her decision had nothing to do with her mother. She told her mother that she was happy in Heaven, greeting animals and pets as they crossed over. Her mother said in wonder, "My daughter was always happiest when she was around animals; I'm so glad she has found this joy in Heaven!"

I was struck by meeting many parents there who had suffered a terrible loss and yet seemed to be able to feel happiness! I was curious about how were they able to feel this way? What did they do to get to such a place of peace? As I dove into those questions in my conversations with other parents, I heard a few describe having a "relationship" with their deceased children. It was here that I began learning that deceased persons shift into spirits of pure energy consciousness. Though they exist on the "other side," they can communicate with us here. I learned about how thin the "veil" is between us and them. So, I bought instructional CDs by Suzanne Giesemann, an evidential medium and retired U.S. Navy commander who spoke at this conference. Her instructions taught one how to deepen one's meditation practice and raise one's energy vibration in order to enhance sensitivity to the spirit world. I wanted to learn how to better sense Ethan's presence in my life and figure out how to have a relationship with him as a spirit son. Despite diligent effort on my part, I could not focus enough in the meditation practice to be able to reach out to Ethan. He seemed to come to me only when *he* wanted to.

I also learned about something called a "soul contract," which refers to the "lessons" we were put on this earth to learn and carry out. Some of us finish our lessons in the afterlife, because evidently that was what we agreed to do even before we were born. At the conference, I bought and read *The Light Between Us* by Laura Lynne Jackson. This book describes how we can come to understand that strong threads of love connect us to those in the afterlife, and if we are open to this connection being real, it can support us as we learn how to build a new relationship with them after their physical death. This concept of love being able to transcend the barrier between human life and spirit life was tremendously comforting and uplifting to me. It gave me hope that my relationship with my son was not really over, it was just changed into something different that I could continue to learn about. I was grieving the loss of my son as I had experienced him for almost twenty-six years on this earth. What if that was all the time he was *supposed* to have on this earth? I alternately tried to accept this strange idea and then I would reject it as not making any sense at all to me.

Chapter 19
NO MERCY

I was dismayed to recognize that I felt resentment toward a couple I met at this conference. During the cocktail reception, they shared with me that their son had died by falling off of a second-story hotel balcony while he was traveling with friends in Europe. They softly explained, "It was simply an accident, an accident that could not have been prevented because it was a result of a problem no one knew anything about." Their son had stood on a balcony that had an unknown faulty support structure and it had simply given way under their son's weight. The hotel gave them a financial settlement, which they donated to a charity in honor of their son. It was clear in their recounting of their story that prior to his death, their son had not failed to launch his young adult life because of an illness, he had not strained the bonds between himself and his family with lying, stealing, and vicious wounding words spoken to them. They were not blaming themselves for anything they felt they did wrong as parents. They were not tortured by judgement of themselves.

As we sat on the patio around the hotel pool after the first day, they described their journey of healing their grief. I sat there listening, almost disbelieving the acceptance I was hearing in their voices and the peace I saw in their faces. They sat across from me lovingly holding hands. How could they have arrived at such a place of peace? When it came time for me to share why I was there, I made up a reason to excuse myself. I simply couldn't tell my story without a thread of self-blame and judgement of myself as a mother laced through it. I showed myself little mercy. I didn't want to reveal this to anyone.

Seeing mercy in Ethan's death was an unexpected concept my brother Rolf brought forward as my siblings from around the country gathered at my home in the days before Ethan's funeral. We all sat around our dining room table with our pastor who was going to conduct Ethan's funeral service. We discussed the possible mercy God bestowed upon Ethan. Rolf said, "It may have been pure mercy that allowed Ethan to die in his car that night after using heroin. He could have lost control of his car as he drove back to La Crosse and hit another car, possibly hurting them, or even worse, killing them." My sister added, "Or, Ethan could have stayed alive and gotten worse… his addiction could have continued on for a long, long time." During that raw first week, I had not contemplated Ethan's death as an act of God's mercy. I remember feeling shock and then resentment at my siblings for even suggesting it. Now, I see it as a possibility that God was merciful to Ethan in calling him home when He did.

According to Merriam-Webster's dictionary, mercy is the gift of withholding harsh treatment that one may have the right to inflict, and instead, showing kindness and compassion. I have been hard on myself all of my life, and after Ethan's death this tendency got worse. A year after his death, I was starting to realize that the difference between me and the couple I met at the conference may have something to do with *me*. In fact, I began to realize that I was becoming consumed by blaming myself. I had catalogued in my mind and heart many interactions and conversations with Ethan that I wished I would have handled differently. I pleaded with myself, "Be merciful towards yourself, Robin! You weren't a perfect parent, and even if you had been, that is no guarantee that Ethan would have lived. You just didn't have that much power in his life. Blaming yourself for how you handled that last conversation with him is, at best, an illusion of your power, and at worst, an arrogant way of thinking." It ended up feeling like I was scolding myself. Talking to myself was not working. My "other Robin" self was silent. Or maybe I wasn't able to hear her. It would take me many more months before I came across a source of help that freed me to be more merciful toward myself.

Chapter 20
DARKNESS

"To suffer our darkness, we must take the pained
and broken parts of ourselves and rock them gently."
– When the Heart Waits, by Sue Monk Kidd

The second year after Ethan died was harder for both Jeff and me than the first. I experienced an escalation of grief and pain as the shock and numbness of the first year faded away. Jeff brought up the possibility of divorce. I started exhibiting PTSD symptoms. I was afraid that I was not okay in a very deep sense. I began a sustained search for any strategy, concept, or intervention that would help me. That second winter I tried to soak away my pain during dark evenings in a hot bath every chance I could get. Water had been a very healing element for me all of my life, until Ethan died and water felt, at times, like being in a sea of grief. Our large triangular shaped bathtub steps up into a corner grotto of Georgia Peach pebbled stones completely covering the walls and ceiling. I felt protected there and able to release, at least for some moments, my mounting pain. I would light a half a dozen candles, bring up a glass of pinot noir, and float in the warm bubbles. Sometimes Jeff would draw the bath for me and sit next to the tub chatting with me, but more often I was alone in the house, as Jeff was periodically spending time living elsewhere or traveling for his new job. I would cry in the steamy bath, sweat and tears mixing together and dripping off of my nose and lips.

I felt my ability to cope was worsening. I found myself drinking more wine as a way to numb myself from the worsening grief. "How hypocritical of you, Robin," I would chastise myself, "to use a substance as a means to cope." I recognized the danger in using that as a coping mechanism, but I didn't really care. I found myself getting more entangled in my definition of myself as being a mother who failed her son. I felt grief about the lonely distance between my husband and me. I felt grief that my connection to my spirit son seemed to have stopped growing…Ethan seemed far away.

I felt myself spiraling downward, or sometimes it seemed inward. My favorite bible verse, Jeremiah 29:11, which had always anchored my confidence in God, now felt like empty promises to me: "For I know the plans I have for you, declares the Lord, plans to prosper you and not to harm you, plans to give you hope and a future." I didn't feel hopeful, nor did I see how God was planning a future that didn't involve more harm and pain.

What I see now is that my faith had been anchored in a more fair-weather view of God. I had trusted in God when our lives seemed golden—everyone healthy, relationships intact, jobs and school going well, lives full of success. I felt prospered and sheltered by God. When tragedy struck our family, I felt He turned away. What I see now is that my pain caused *me* to move away from His care and protection.

I was becoming aware that I was not going to heal on my own. I could not heal myself. I asked myself, "If a client came to you asking for help with this type of loss and emotional pain surrounding the loss, what would you say to her?" That's it! I thought, the first thing I need to do is ask for help. I didn't need to know what help exactly. What I instinctively knew was that I needed to reach outside of myself for intervention, guidance—please, even some magic. I felt a strong drive toward trying *anything* that might help me. I was not sure what would make the difference. I wasn't sure of much anymore.

What followed in my life, for more than eighteen long months, were interventions of many different types from many kind and wise people. I know now that God didn't turn away from me, he sent hope and a future for me through these people.

But when I thought I was finally healed, I was wrong. I had one of the hardest parts of my journey still ahead of me. God may have planned that, too.

PART THREE

Chapter 21
HEALING PRACTICES

I recalled that the medium I had seen a year ago suggested that I meet with someone called an Emotion Code Practitioner to obtain help in releasing the judgement and self-blame I harbored. I decided to meet with her—why not try this? I felt a bit skeptical about the effectiveness of this intervention looking at it through my psychotherapist lens, but at this point I was willing to try anything. I learned about a strategy to support the body's natural ability to rid itself from toxic energy of negative emotions trapped in the body from *The Emotion Code*, written by Bradley Nelson, MD. I met with a practitioner, Kathy, a kind and gentle woman, several times. My husband even met with her twice, and my daughter did once as well. Damaging emotions can also be passed down from one's parents, and even from previous generations. She told me that I carried an "inherited emotion" of feeling "failure as a mother" from many generations before me. The burden of carrying these emotions within one's body and spirit can cause physical, emotional and spiritual ill health. She told me that my spirit was disconnected from my body, and that I was isolated from my own self and from the Divine Source within me. I had noticed this growing disconnection within myself during my yoga practice. I tried hard to cover this up, because I felt like a bit of a fraud when I encouraged my yoga students to reconnect with their spirits and the spark of the Divine within them during their yoga practice.

She utilized a fascinating intervention that involved my DNA from a hair on my head, a pendulum, and magnetism. She recommended that I repeat positive affirmations as she worked with me to release my negative emotion of blaming myself for Ethan's death. We crafted this affirmation together: *"I am not responsible for others' actions and feelings. I am responsible only for my own health and happiness."* This affirmation was hard for me to accept as a mom. We mothers are conditioned to feel responsible for our children, their little bodies, their needs, and their hurts. When Deva and Ethan were young, I made very sure they napped when they were tired, I dressed them in warm clothes when it was cold, I fed them healthy food when they were hungry, I loved over them when they were hurt in their bodies or in their hearts. I urged them to take good care of themselves as they got older. I encouraged them to try hard at what mattered to them and was right in God's eyes. I was certainly imperfect in doing all of that mothering. All of us moms are imperfect. I could accept that level of normal imperfection. But Ethan had a mom whose training was in the field of mental health and substance abuse, and he died from his addiction. That was hard for me to accept.

It surprised me that my feeling responsible for him clung to me so tenaciously. I explored this. As a therapist, I do not feel responsible for my clients' health—much less, their *lives*. I see my role as helping *them* to be responsible for their health and healing. I think the fact that Ethan's illness started while he was still in adolescence, and dogged him into his transition into adulthood, never allowed us as parents to experience him as an efficacious independent adult. I couldn't truly relinquish caretaking of him as his illness worsened while he grew into his mid-twenties, because he often didn't exhibit the adult behaviors associated with his numerical age.

A symptom of addiction is that it disrupts emotional maturation at the level one was at when the disease of addiction starts.

Ethan often made decisions as though he was still an adolescent. On top of that, his decisions became governed by an addicted brain. We saw that in him and accepted it as part of his illness. But how does a mother stand by, watching one's adult child make harmful decisions—even life-threatening ones—and not want to leap in and protect their child? Leap in with just enough protection to make sure he stayed alive until he learned how to live his life free of substances?

I couldn't let go of the drive to keep mothering him as I have naturally done with my daughter. We watched Deva as she launched herself successfully into adulthood. Certainly, she made mistakes, but none were life-threatening or unable to be fixed. We observed her taking steps toward pursuing a master's degree, building healthy friendships, leaving a relationship with a man who didn't meet her needs, and forming a new one with a man who would eventually become her husband. We've experienced her developing an adult relationship with us as her parents, which is delightful and deeply satisfying.

All parents desire these types of outcomes as they parent their child. When this doesn't occur, or, unimaginably, our child dies, the wound to our hearts can be almost too hard to bear. In addition to this wound, I also felt that I somehow let Ethan down in my responsibility to him as a mother.

So, the other affirmation I was to repeat was targeted to helping myself show forgiveness toward myself: *"I was the best mother I could be to Ethan. His father and I set healthy boundaries for ourselves on December 26th, 2016 in our last conversation with him. I have happy memories of being with Ethan. I learned so much from having Ethan as our son. I feel at peace. Ethan's life ended how it ended, and I let go of that. Ethan made choices for his life, and I accept that. I respect that we are all free to make our own choices."*

Mantras, like affirmations, are a Buddhist concept that aid in achieving a meditative state and can eventually lead to self-transformation if repeated regularly over time. I have used mantras in my yoga practice. Even the Disney movie *Moana* utilized this powerful tool. When this movie came out in early 2017, I watched it at least a dozen times. I was so drawn to the strength that the main character, Moana, derived from the mantra that her grandmother gave her and told her to repeat out loud whenever she felt her confidence waver. After watching *Moana* several times with me, my soul sister JeMae gave me this mantra to repeat when I felt the piercing pain of feeling alone in my grief: *"I am Robin. I am safe. I am okay. If I need help, I will ask for it, and it will come."* Later, she suggested another mantra to repeat as I doubted the directive I had received to write my story: *"I am doing the right thing in sharing my story. I will not give up. I will embrace my doubts and send them on their way. I will trust my heart and forge ahead."*

As a therapist, I believe in the healing power of speaking our truth and of having that truth listened to and gently held by another. This process of speaking and being heard helps to foster change and growth in one's self. While it was helpful to more clearly identify why my negative belief was so entrenched inside of myself, I wasn't ready to fully own the truth of the affirmation: I was the best mother I could have been to Ethan. The strength I received from my affirmations faded. The affirmations were positive, but my heart was not yet truly receptive to embrace these messages.

To further explore how I could forgive myself, I returned to the book *Radical Forgiveness*. Colin Tipping's premise is that we all "play out victimhood in every aspect of our lives, convincing ourselves that victim consciousness is absolutely fundamental to the human con-dition." The challenge that he posits for us is to "stop ignoring the lesson that Jesus taught us—that there are no victims…Jesus gave us a powerful demonstration of what transforming the victim arche-type means" in his death on the cross (pg. xvi—xvii). Contemplating the message of this book jolted me. I wondered if I was journeying through my grief from a victim stance when I repeated in my heart that, "It wasn't fair that Ethan didn't live, when others with worse and longer heroin addictions are still alive!" And this: "It isn't fair that my husband has abandoned me when I most need him!" And this, too: "It isn't fair that some of my friends and family aren't here for me the way I need them to be!" And most ashamedly this: "It isn't fair that Ethan couldn't or wouldn't use all of the treatment, support, and love he got from us and his myriad of providers so that he wouldn't have died! Ethan, why didn't you heal with all the resources you had? The lessons of self-care I taught you—to ask for help, to ask for what you need, to shout out loud what it is you want, like you did before you got sick! You used to be so strong and force-ful—even demanding—when it came to you going after what you wanted. Where did all of that steely strength in you *go*?"

I had not considered that in my grief a woman was buried who might be thinking like a victim. This was not the kind of woman I wanted to be. I wanted to be forgiving, strong, self-aware, and psychologically healthy. Certainly not a woman who held onto such unhealthy emotions like shame or feeling victimized by a tragic outcome that was "unfair." Or worse, blaming my dead son! No wonder I felt stuck. I felt stuck in gut-punching, breath-stealing, joy-sucking blame. Blaming Ethan's providers, especially his two long-term therapists. Blaming even Ethan. Blaming myself through questions, sharp as weedy thistles pricking at me—"Robin, why did you support him getting off of Methadone? Why didn't you let him come home and get a job and treatment here as he asked that day after Christmas?" I was learning that forgiving myself was the hardest type of forgiveness to accomplish.

I decided to consult another practitioner, Caitria, from Connected Healing, who specialized in healing practices from the traditions of Chinese medicine and acupuncture. After hearing my story and the relief I was looking for, she gave me an acupuncture treatment and some self-care suggestions, which made me roll my eyes internally. I knew all about those suggestions already. Then she said, *"Robin, there is grace for you in vulnerability."* Surprised, I thought, "What a strange thing for her to say out of the blue like that!" But I listened and thought about that word—vulnerability. I had not really thought about that word in a long time. The first thing I do with a challenging word is see what Merriam-Webster thinks. Ethan and I did this many times over the years when we tried to stump each other with hard words. I learned vulnerability comes from the Latin word "vulnerare" which means "to wound." So, being vulnerable means being open to being wounded? No way. I didn't want more of that.

Much later in my journey I would remember her words as I allowed—and even challenged myself—to be vulnerable with my husband. I would experience the grace of God and spiritual healing in that practice then.

I wasn't ready to be that vulnerable now.

Instead, I repeated Loving Kindness Meditations for myself and for those whom I wanted to forgive, to lessen my blame of myself and them: "May I be healthy, may I be happy, may I peaceful, may I be whole. May Jeff be healthy, may Jeff be happy, may Jeff be peaceful, may Jeff be whole."

And I prayed. I asked God to erase from my heart the blame I carried. I found myself screaming until my throat was raw one morning alone in my living room, looking at the cedar chest covered with the mementos from Ethan's funeral. My child was not supposed to die before me! Wrung out, I reached for my Bible and randomly opened it up to Romans, Chapter 8. My eyes landed on verse 26: "The Spirit helps us in our weakness. For we do not know what to pray for as we ought, but the Spirit himself intercedes for us with groanings too deep for words." Was I praying for the wrong thing? Perhaps God wasn't going to release me from my blame; I needed to do that work myself. At the very least, I longed to feel the solidarity of God's Spirit groaning with me.

Sally from my women's group suggested I get away and attend a spiritual retreat. She told me about a place deep in the woods of central Wisconsin, called The Christine Center. This special place is as close to an emotional ICU as I have experienced in my journey. It was founded by the Franciscan Sisters for the purpose of spiritual transformation. During those first two years after Ethan's death, I attended four different retreats there, experiencing its healing energy in spring, fall, and winter. One of them was a yoga and meditation retreat. During that three-day weekend I felt so nourished. Nourished by the wonderfully healthy food, which to my surprise I felt hungry for. I ate three meals each day, something I hadn't done since Ethan died. Nourished by the forest, bathing me in peace and calm. Nourished by the restorative yoga practices, so unlike the challenging yoga I typically practiced. Nourished by the long periods of silence asked of the retreatants to observe. Nourished by staying in a cozy hermitage, which was a tiny one-room cabin tucked into the woods within walking distance of the retreat center. Each one had lyrical names like Sun-Catcher, MoonCatcher, Joy, Earth, Peace, Rumi, St. Francis, Basil. The one assigned to me was named Gabriel. Gabriel, one of God's angels. I imagined an angel watched over me as I slept peacefully with no nightmares in my hermitage.

On the second day of the retreat, the leaders gave each one of us an oracle card from the "Our Lady the Virgin Mother" oracle card collection. There are forty-four cards in the collection, and each one of the retreatants was given the card that was meant for them to focus on during the retreat. An "oracle" is a person considered to be able to provide wise and insightful counsel and prophetic predictions or precognition of the future. I received the card of "Our Lady of the Dark Mysteries." I suddenly couldn't swallow as I read my card. I wanted to roll up my mat and drive the three hours straight back home. I came for succor and received *this* message to contemplate?! Why was I given this card out of all the cards I could have received?

It read: *"If you are encountering the dark face of Mother Mary, sometimes known as the Black Madonna, you are being initiated into a powerful spiritual consciousness, and will be granted the ability to find love, healing, and peace from the darkest of human experiences...If you are called to this path at this particular time of your life, it is because it will serve you most...She calls you through pain when pleasure would not suffice. She calls through suffering because it will break open your heart into greater capacity for bliss and rapture. All that you give will be returned to you as grace and miracles. Do not turn away...there is transformative healing that is happening through your pain...She will not let you go…you are not alone and she calls you to her in increasing crisis and struggle, until you pay attention…She will hold the container for you to feel, and release emotions—even though they can be so painful that you may feel as though they are going to tear you into pieces as you feel them…you need to make peace with your challenges, instead of holding guilt or shame about those challenges you face…"*

To be *held* while I felt and released my darkest emotion of shame—was that what I needed in my deepest self? When I read the word "shame," it jolted me deep in my solar plexus. My most honest self prodded me to admit that I did feel shame—shame, that despite my knowledge and training, my son died. Such a dirty emotion. So black and toxic. The dark side of pridefulness. Such a sin for me to feel shame about the illness and death of my son. Over and over I whispered, "I am so sorry, Ethan, that I allowed shame to creep into my heart. I am not embarrassed by you or your illness. God, please help me…"

I frankly did not want to be burned by the fire of spiritual "transformation," or face "shame," or "pay attention." I just wanted to feel less desperately sad.

But there was no shortcut out of this. No way to go but through.

Chapter 22
MY CO-DESTINY

I felt so sad that I would never watch Ethan rise above his addiction and spread his own unique personality into the world. I know that it is my mother's heart wanting—perhaps selfishly—to see my child be successful. Isn't that what all parents want to see in our children? I needed to re-define "success" in my mind regarding my son's life. Participating in making Ethan's Run Against Addiction come alive with such a wonderful outcome got me thinking that this was a way that Ethan's spirit was making an impact. It was making a difference in others' lives. We could continue this work—make Ethan's Run an annual event—and accomplish some of the work Ethan might have done if he were still alive. In the year before he died, he had talked about enrolling at Viterbo University in La Crosse to become a Substance Abuse counselor, because he wanted to help others in their recovery.

In my reading on parental grief work, I discovered a master's thesis titled *Co-Destiny* written by Joseph E. Kasper, MD. Dr. Kasper's son, Ryan, died at seventeen, and he deeply struggled to make sense of this tragedy, like all of us parents do each in our own way. He wanted to do more than survive his loss; he wanted to learn from it as well. He wanted to pursue "post-traumatic growth" after Ryan's death, not just heal from his grief. He created the concept of "co-destiny" to describe this process. He first defined it as the interweaving of one's deceased child's destiny with that of the parent's own destiny. Many of the 70,237 persons who died of a drug overdose in the United States in 2017 were still young adults and still active in a parent/child relationship (The National Institute on Drug Abuse). Their young lives were cut short by their illness, and their purpose and mission as adults on this Earth were seemingly never realized. There are so many parents mourning the loss of their child's destiny being fulfilled. I deeply resonated with Dr. Kasper's concept. I, too, wanted to see Ethan's death as more than a random senseless event, and I wanted to learn what I could do with my life moving forward that would honor my son's life.

Dr. Kasper's definition of co-destiny includes this very challenging step: "Achieve complete acceptance of their child's death, through understanding the meaning and purpose of their child's life..." (pg. 41). Could I really accept Ethan's death? Honestly, I was not sure that I was able to do that or if I even wanted to accept it. Accepting his death was acknowledging the absolute finality of his life being over on this Earth. I knew I did want to move past focusing on the lonely, terrible way he had died, in a McDonald's parking lot. I wanted to understand the reasons—Joe Kasper refers to them as "the benefits"—why Ethan was given to me and my husband as our son for the years he was in his physical body. I wanted to be able to celebrate the purpose of Ethan's life. I wanted to live my life with the feeling that my son was, and is still, a gift to me and to others. I didn't want to continue to associate Ethan's death with me feeling like a victim of God's indifference to my prayers for my son's health. That view separated me from God, and Ethan, too.

But, there was something keeping me stuck. I was aware of something being wrong, missing, off with me. I saw a new medium, Jake, and through him, I asked Ethan, "Did I do anything wrong as your mom?"

His answer was, "No, Mom! I know you and Dad loved me; you did everything you could to help me. I am sorry that you are so sad. I am doing very well here; please stop crying, Mom."

I found myself unable to stop crying during that reading, so desperate to understand how I could accept the reality of losing Ethan. Ethan said, "There is nothing you could have done about my drug addiction. My choices and mistakes were on me and me alone. It was more than that I chose to take so many drugs, it was that I also chose a lifestyle that I thought I could control, but I found I couldn't." Jake explained that, "Some of us don't learn our lessons in this physical life, and so need to continue learning them in the next life—except, maybe, if you are Mother Teresa," he said with a smile.

Becoming still again, listening to Ethan's presence in the room, Jake said, "Your son has the mind of a poet—words were important to him. He is singing to me and playing a guitar; was he a musician?" I said, "Yes, music was like food to him."

Jake went on to say that while, "We live and breathe in a milieu of oxygen, our loved ones on the other side exist in the milieu of purest love. He *is* pure love now and is greeting and loving other young people coming to the other side from a drug overdose. In fact, he has met other musicians who are teaching him how to care for those who cross over due to addiction." Jake said that Ethan wants me to do only one thing: "Love yourself and everyone in your life like you loved me, Mom."

I didn't really take in that last message from Ethan until a year later when I listened to the recording of that fifty minute reading again as I was writing this story. I heard Ethan's words again, and could hardly breathe. That was, in fact, the exact lesson I needed to learn. To love. To love Jeff, my husband, despite his betrayal. To love myself despite my judgment of having failed as a mom. To love others when they let me down and didn't meet my expectations. But at the time of that reading, I wasn't able to fully absorb this message from Ethan. Like his dad and I always said about Ethan, he learned things the hard way. I, too, learned this lesson of loving myself the hard way.

It was not lost on me at the first Ethan's Run event that I was entreating hundreds of participants to let go of shame and stigma, and I couldn't seem to do it for myself. Yet when I watched the media interview of Jeff and me after the race, I saw how moved I seemed about the outcome, that I smiled and appeared even joyful. No one would guess what I was feeling on the inside. People kept saying how awesome the race was, and that I must be, "riding a wave of pride in all of the good that flowed from this event." I did, but I also felt a tremendous letdown within myself as the weeks went by afterwards. I had felt closer to Ethan while so many of us had worked together to plan the event. My heart had lifted up and soared seeing his name on all of the white race t-shirts, written in his favorite color of deep blue. When one's loved one dies, as time goes on, you hear and see their name less and less. However, at this event, my son's name was emblazoned on seven-hundred and sixty-four t-shirts!

I fervently thanked God for blessing me with the strength and motivation to carry forward Ethan's story, his passion for life, his compassion and interest in others. I felt this was a way to keep Ethan's destiny alive. I began to understand that Ethan's spirit is active here and doing some of that work himself. I didn't need to do it all. We could do it together. Perhaps I wasn't in the sea alone.

Ethan seemed to be communicating this to all of us when suddenly three birds began circling the flag that the runners and walkers turned to face with hands on their hearts during the singing of the National Anthem before the starting pistol went off. Just as the last notes of the song rang out, the birds lifted up Heavenward.

Chapter 23
BRAINSPOTTING

Soon after Ethan's Run was finished, Jeff told me over the phone while out of the country on a business trip that he wanted to discuss a divorce. I felt shell-shocked.

With the threat of another loss looming over me, I no longer had the energy to keep the trauma I had experienced during the many years of Ethan's worsening addiction pushed down inside of me. Perhaps that was happening for Jeff, too. I pleaded with him to meet with our pastor, the pastor that married Deva and put Ethan to rest. We met with Pastor Rob, and Jeff agreed to re-commit to our marriage. Yet, I felt, at best, an uneasy sense of only warding off disaster for the time being.

One summer evening several weeks after that meeting, I was home alone after work and was swimming laps in our pool, trying to let go of my worry and fear. Suddenly, in the middle of a lap, I was hit with such a wave of intense grief over Ethan's death that I couldn't swim another stroke. My arms couldn't seem to propel me forward, much less keep me afloat in the deep end. Water was my comfortable, healing space, but I barely made it to the side of the pool, gasping, and I clung to the edge sobbing with such hacking sounds that I didn't even recognize the sound of my own voice. What was happening to me? I suddenly felt burning on my body the physical scars of my delivering Ethan into this world, and the fresh wounds burning in my heart of grieving Ethan's leaving this world. I literally felt my heart was breaking, my body drowning in grief.

If my body could talk to me, it would be saying that I needed an anchor. When we are in a crisis swirling around us, we need to find an anchor to hold on to and wait for the violent motion to slow so that we can finally steady ourselves. I didn't see an anchor I could grab hold of.

God guides by what He provides, but also by what He *withholds*. In the absence of having what we think we need, we learn, grow, and change. Jeff was clearly not able to be an anchor for me. Nor could I be an anchor for him. I knew I needed to ask for professional help. I felt close to a breakdown. Radhe, who again was an angel in my life, suggested a relatively new body-centered treatment for trauma called brainspotting.

I was aware that I had been exhibiting increasing signs of Post-Traumatic Stress Disorder (PTSD) for a number of months. I remember the first time I became aware of the PTSD. One night, a group of eight of us friends were sitting outside on a patio enjoying the spring air. Suddenly, the air conditioner unit near the patio kicked on. I leaped up out of my chair and dropped my glass. No one else even seemed to notice the unit turning on.

I struggled driving to familiar places, sometimes even getting lost. I had several minor car accidents, such as driving into a light pole or backing into a tree. I grew anxious. I was clumsy, tripping often. I began wearing flats to work, afraid I might fall in my normal high heels as I walked back and forth on campus for meetings. I kept bumping into furniture that had been in the same place in my home and office, causing ugly bruising and cuts on my shins and thighs. I was overwhelmed with responsibilities of self-care, such as showering. When a shower had to include all three tasks of washing my hair, shaving, and removing makeup, I became so distressed that I avoided showering for days at a time. I stopped shaving, I washed my hair only when putting it in a ponytail no longer could disguise its lankness, and I recycled my makeup for days. I struggled to decide what to wear to work. I found myself having to concentrate harder on tasks. My memory, normally sharp, was unreliable in situations that I experienced as stressful. I began to have flashbacks of seeing Ethan unconscious, lying in the woods on the Root River Parkway near our house. A sound sleeper all of my life, when I began to have nightmares, I finally took an online quiz for PTSD. I already knew what it would reveal, but I needed to see it in black and white. I scored at the "severe" level.

Brainspotting proved to be a treatment that was the beginning of finally healing that which I didn't even know needed healing within me. I began seeing a psychotherapist, Josh, who specialized in brainspotting and treating trauma, twice a week beginning in July of 2018. In addition to PTSD, I learned that I was suffering from something called "traumatic grief," which is different than uncomplicated grief. Stored up trauma—called "unprocessed trauma"—coupled with grief becomes traumatic grief. I couldn't fully heal from Ethan's death until my stored up traumatic memories were processed in my brain. I could *experience* the support of my grief counselor, my grief support group, and all of the other healing practices that I had been pursuing for the past eighteen months, but I couldn't fully *integrate* the benefits from those interventions until I processed the trauma I had suffered. Trauma suffered, particularly, in situations where I had felt helpless. For example, I recalled after Ethan's first suicide attempt at age eighteen, he was hooked up to a ventilator in the ICU to breathe. I had matched each one of my breaths to his, sitting up in a chair next to his bed all night long. Feeling completely helpless, I poured love into each breath, praying he would please, please, please wake up. I didn't know what else to do.

Jeff and I as a parenting team had responded to other very scary situations with Ethan, like the one in the ICU, in which we felt helpless. I had not been aware of how many traumatic memories were buried deep beneath my conscious awareness. They had been piling up, one on top of the other, over the years. There was no safe space in those years to process them. We were always readying ourselves for the next crisis. These unprocessed memories were hampering me to the point that I struggled to even function. Josh commented, after I described Ethan's suicide attempts, mental health and drug abuse history, "It seems Ethan was in a hurry to leave his body." Jeff and I had been so focused on making sure he stayed alive in his body! Trauma resulted from the intersection of those two realities.

Having been a competitive long-distance runner all my life, I believe that effort produces results. My dad raised me to believe in the power of sustained intention backed up by sustained striving. I was frustrated that my sustained efforts to move past my grief—by advocating for others suffering from opioid addiction, facilitating the GRASP group, speaking to community agencies, working on being forgiving and merciful toward myself, journaling, consulting with the Emotion Code practitioner, meeting with mediums, prayer, and meditation—had started me on my way but hadn't gotten me to the full peaceful acceptance of Ethan's death that I yearned for. The opioid epidemic had become a cause through which I used my gifts as a healer and a leader to do good work for others, but I was compromising myself in all of this effort. I needed to stop trying so hard to heal—or, at least, try *differently*. Brainspotting proved to be the intervention that helped me break through the stored traumatic memories in my brain, and took me to the next level in my healing process.

For me, brainspotting is like psychotherapeutic "savasana." Every yoga class ends in savasana, which is a Sanskrit word for corpse pose. This pose is one where the body is completely still and in a state of non-efforting. I instruct my yoga students at the end of their practice to *"sink into your mat, allow it to hold you, allow yourself to just breathe. No effort is needed at this point in your practice. Allow yourself to be completely at rest. Let go of effort and give in to this time of restoration."* At this point in my grief journey, I was ready to heed my own instructions to my yoga students and let go of effort. In brainspotting, one is still and allows the brain do its own healing, trusting in one's brain to know what needs to be healed and how. I have always relied on my cognitive brain to do what I wanted it to do. We all take our brains for granted, until they stop working so well. In the aftermath of Ethan's death, my brain seemed to gradually retreat and withdraw into itself until I couldn't ignore that I needed to give my brain permission to do exactly that—retreat into itself. So, I embraced this brainspotting work with Josh. Savasana for my traumatized brain.

David Grand, PhD, who created this intervention, writes in his book *Brainspotting: The Revolutionary New Therapy for Rapid and Effective Change* that "The brain is an incredible processing machine that digests and organizes everything we experience. But trauma can overwhelm the brain's processing capacity, leaving behind pieces of the trauma, frozen in an unprocessed state" (pg. 3). God created the brain to be the amazing organ that it is, normally solving most challenges we face in life. But when my PTSD symptoms appeared, my brain was trying to tell me that it was stuck in its healing. We humans don't have the ability to shake off a traumatic experience in the way that I watched my little puppy do when she tumbled over the stone retaining wall in our backyard—she got up, stunned, shook herself all up and down her body several times, and then trotted off to continue her exploration of the backyard. Grand maintains that when the brain is stuck in this way, "either the brain can't locate the problem inside itself, or it knows where the problem is but doesn't know how to untangle it. Such unsolvable problems are often trauma based" (pg. 93). I realized that many traumatic memories during Ethan's illness were still tangled inside me. I felt heavy and weighted down by them.

Brainspotting refers to the carefully chosen spot my therapist helps me locate to gaze at. One way he does this is by observing where my eyes feel drawn to look as I recall a traumatic memory. Grand explains that the brain "*knows* where to look." While gazing at this spot, I focus on the sensations in my body that rise up as I recall, for example, the traumatic memory of Ethan lying there in the ICU dependent on the breathing machine. While I could remember being in that extremely fearful situation and feeling helpless to do anything about it, that memory became inaccessible inside my brain for me to cognitively heal until I brainspotted it.

I recalled the hissing and clicking of the machine, the tube down my son's throat, the utter stillness of his body on the hospital bed as if he were dead. As I became more activated by this memory, I experienced a swollen throat and couldn't swallow, an aching chest as if my heart was pressing on its heart wall so it could jump out and leap into my son's heart and infuse it with love and health. My hands couldn't stop curling and uncurling, wanting to reach out and comfort him. My shoulders felt bowed down and heavily burdened as if I was trying to carry him to safety.

I focused on my body's activation while continuing to gaze at the identified spot. Now the brain is able to focus on the buried traumatic activation and begins to process it. This processing doesn't require any talking at all. In fact, it, "doesn't happen in a cognitive, linear fashion. It is a deep brain process and its complexity is way beyond the reach and comprehension of our conscious awareness...when our conscious brain wisely accepts its limitations and trusts our deeper brain, it is led down a path of deeper healing and resolution," (pg. 94). So, that is why I couldn't *think* my way to being healed.

In addition, while the brainspotting session is occurring, one is encouraged to listen to "Bio-Lateral" sounds of nature or healing music through headphones at a very low level. I choose waves every time I experience brainspotting because the sound of water is very soothing to me. These sounds move back and forth from ear to ear, gently stimulating the right and left sides of the brain to aid in the healing process.

I began bringing traumatic memories from all the years of helping Ethan to my therapy sessions. I would brainspot those with Josh. Brainspotting can be used to treat PTSD, as well as depression, anxiety, addiction, physical pain, chronic illness, and more. I needed relief from my growing PTSD symptoms. I would feel tired afterward, and often tearful, but I was willing to do whatever it would take to bring peace into my aching heart and soul. Dr. Grand refers to this as turning "lead into gold" within one's brain.

Chapter 24
BREAKING POINT

Twenty-one months after Ethan died, I broke. After returning from an invitation to speak about "Ethan's Story" at the second Opioid Crisis Congress on September 26th, 2018, in Washington D.C., I felt myself fractured to the point that I couldn't keep the pieces of myself together any longer. The final trigger had been a terrible experience I had the last day Jeff and I were in D.C.

Early that morning I had gone for a run on the Rock Creek Parkway near our hotel. After my turnaround point, I heard sirens coming up behind me. This was always a trigger for me, as I associate sirens with the ambulance ride I took with Ethan when he was raced to a trauma hospital, sirens screaming, after his first suicide attempt at age eighteen. What I wasn't prepared for as I rounded the curve of the parkway, was seeing the white Toyota Corolla abandoned sideways in the middle of the road, front door wide open. I suddenly stopped, breathing hard.

Ethan drove a white Corolla. I watched the police officers looking for something, or maybe someone, in the thick growth hugging the Rock Creek. They were setting up barricades to close down the parkway. Suddenly I flashed back to the day nine years ago that we—my husband, my daughter, her friend, Ethan's girlfriend, the Greenfield Police—were all desperately looking for Ethan in the woods along the Root River Parkway. Seeing the white Corolla on the Rock Creek Parkway now nine years later, I felt like I was back in that horrific search for Ethan in the thick growth along the Root River. We were racing against time to find him, because all of his medications, the Tylenol, and alcohol were gone from our house.

Standing there, utter helplessness flooded me. What if they couldn't find who they were looking for? My heart pounded, my throat felt tight with fear, my hands clenched and unclenched. I knew I had to go help look for the young man (I assumed) that had fled his Corolla so suddenly. I started jogging towards the scene, only to stop as I got closer. I said to myself, "Robin—are you crazy? They aren't going to let you help! Leave, leave, leave, Robin! This is not about Ethan." But standing there, my flashback of that terrible day took over. I couldn't move. Fear surged throughout my body as the image of my unconscious son lying on the dirt trail in the woods filled my mind. I saw the white froth dried around his mouth, the awkward angle into which his body was twisted. I watched in my mind's eye the paramedic jabbing Ethan with a shot of Narcan. Nothing I had been practicing so far helped me in this very moment. All I could do was breathe and wait for my shaking to subside.

I cried as I backed away from the frightening scene and then slowly walked back to the hotel. I irrationally felt I was abandoning Ethan by leaving this scene. I felt a tremendous sense of fear that the person the police were looking for was going to die. I understood that I was reacting from the place I was in nine years ago. I tried to shake it off, but I couldn't.

I described the scene to my husband when I returned to the hotel room, still very upset. He told me to "let it go, you know it wasn't Ethan who left that car." The therapist side of me rationally did know that to be true, because I understood the impact of PTSD on my brain, but my body didn't. My body felt like I was again living through Ethan almost dying that first time. Jeff's training as a police officer led him to react stoically in many of these traumatic situations. This is normal, and even advantageous, for law enforcement and first responders in general. However, traumatic memories don't necessarily go away because we tell ourselves to let them go, to push them away, or to bury them deep inside. Jeff would start brainspotting treatment of his own a year later. It would only be then that he started to heal his buried grief around our son's death.

My therapist felt that my breaking down was a "positive sign." It meant I was finally allowing myself to acknowledge my exhaustion, my pain, my inability to keep pushing, pushing, pushing myself. I had no choice but to listen to myself. I decided to take an extended leave of absence from my job. I had been working more than full-time for twenty-nine years in the demanding field of Behavioral Health either as a provider or a leader. My pace had not slowed down—in fact, it had only increased with my promotion—since Ethan died, with the exception of the three weeks I had taken off immediately after he died. My waking hours in the past twenty-one months had been scheduled to the minute.

Chapter 25
STILLED

"I will not be afraid to be still. I will sit gently with myself and be still."
- Healing After Loss, Daily Meditations for Working Through Grief,
Martha Whitmore Hickman

I was suddenly not scheduled. I was stilled. I found myself sleeping more than six hours a night, then more than eight hours, and sometimes even ten hours. I hadn't slept like this since our children had been born. I didn't speak for many hours on some days. I moved slowly, in stark contrast with my habit of rushing. I didn't put my fingers on a keyboard for weeks at a time. I spent time with my husband having lunch in our sunny dining room, chatting. I ate slowly. Jeff surprised me with a rescued puppy from Texas, called Roxy Rose. An unconditional gift from him to me. She brought joy into our grieving home. She made us laugh and have something to care for. It felt like we were a family with Roxy in our lives. We walked Roxy together. We sat together on the couch in front of the fire, sometimes talking about Ethan, sometimes not. I was grateful for these moments of grace between us.

I was finally trying to take better care of myself, per the instructions of a tarot card reader I met in D.C. After the conference I spoke at was concluded, Jeff and I stayed three more days, walking around neighborhoods we had once hung out in when we lived in D.C. before we were married. We wandered into Georgetown and walked past a door painted in a soft lavender color. Out of the corner of my eye, I noticed there was a small silver sign that said "Tarot Card Readings" on the door. We strolled past it, and then I suddenly stopped and said to Jeff, "I am supposed to go back to that house with the purple door and get a tarot card reading." I didn't have any idea what that was, but I listened to that voice in my head and knocked on the door.

A conservatively dressed woman opened the door. I had expected a woman with a flowing skirt and jingly jewelry. I naively asked, "Are you available to do a reading for me now?" She warmly laughed and said, "Normally, I do not provide walk-in service, but I just received a cancellation for this time, so please, come in and sit down."

She led me into a quiet, softly lit, small room. The energy in the room felt calm and safe. There was the sound of trickling water from a small fountain in the room. With no information from me other than my first name, she turned over certain cards on the table between us and then began speaking, "You are some sort of a healer, a therapist, perhaps? You are giving too much of yourself away. You are on the cusp of much change in your life. But you are hesitating doing what your intuition says you should do for yourself."

She paused for several breaths after turning over another card. Then lifting her eyes to me she said, "You have suffered a great loss of a loved one, someone very close to you, so close that it is as if your souls were connected. Who was this person to you?"

I said, "My son, Ethan, who died twenty-one months ago."

She told me, "You must believe that Ethan is all around you and with you."

Suddenly tearful, I said, "I don't feel him around me very often at all. I don't understand why!"

With exquisite tenderness in her voice, she put her hand on mine and said, "You are not taking care of yourself the way you need to in your grieving. Your husband is too distracted right now to love you the way you want to be loved. You need to mother *yourself*, perhaps travel somewhere healing—I think California."

After some more gentle sharing, I hugged her, and then I stepped out into the late afternoon sunshine where my husband was patiently waiting for me. We didn't talk as we continued our walk that last day in the city where we were so in love thirty-four years earlier.

As a student of yoga for eleven years, I have worked to develop a regular meditation practice. But after Ethan died, I was unable to meditate. Grief swooped in when I tried to meditate. Waves of sorrow made it hard to quiet my mind. I gave up trying to meditate, and I read instead. Reading has been a source of comfort and distraction for me since I was a young girl eager to read everything I could find about horses, especially the Walter Farley horse books. My sister and I shared the entire *Trixie Belden* series, and all of the *Nancy Drew* mysteries. As I settled into my leave of absence, I read everything I could find about grief. I sat with those authors and their stories of their grief journeys and felt comforted when I recognized myself. I felt we had a shared experience. I wasn't crazy, after all, to feel such pain. They felt it too. I felt alone in my marriage regarding my regret about so much concerning Ethan: my remorse over boundaries we had to set, my self-blame over missing cues within Ethan that he was in danger of relapsing. Jeff did not share these feelings. We had not been able to bridge this difference between us. These authors companioned me into a less lonely place in my grieving.

While on medical leave that fall, it was becoming clearer to me as I assessed my workplace environment through the lens of the distance I now had, that going back to work may not be a healthy or viable option for me. I wrestled with the enormity of leaving an eighteen-year career at my current employer. It felt like another loss. Losing my son, and now my job? Putting that decision aside when it was overwhelming to consider, I sat and read in stillness for hours on end, my puppy sleeping on my lap.

"The Lord will fight for you: you need only to be still."
- Exodus 14:14

After some weeks, I was also able to sit quietly in prayer. At last, I was not being angry at God, or asking anything of Him. It was more like a running stream of conversation with God. I had started a gratitude practice many years ago with my daughter when she was a preteen, which I tried to continue over the years. It had stopped after Ethan's death. Now, when I could think of nothing to say to God, I would try to name something I was grateful for. When I couldn't think of anything to be grateful for, I said nothing to God. I just sat there with Him. He seemed okay with that. This is how God started to lead me back to a relationship with Him. A gift.

I continued my journaling, which I started after Ethan died, writing daily about all that was on my heart during this time of my life. I would often pause, pen in hand, resting on my open journal, and then I would become aware that twenty minutes had gone by. I grew more comfortable sitting in stillness with no goal or expectation for any outcome, or any measure of productivity. I gradually grew able to sit and just breathe, in and out, in and out. I regained my mediation practice. This was not my doing, but another gift to me from God.

I started to feel like God perhaps had never left me, I just needed to be stilled enough to realize that it was perhaps me, in my anger and grief, who had left Him.

Chapter 26
MY SACRED CONTRACT

"Be patient toward all that is unsolved in your heart,
and try to love the questions themselves..."
- Rainer Maria Rilke

I read *Comfortable with Uncertainty* by Pema Chodron and pondered her view as an American Buddhist nun that "We try to control the uncontrollable by looking for security and predictability, always hoping to be comfortable and safe. But the truth is that we can never avoid uncertainty" (pg. 5). Given that there was so much uncertainty in my life, I tried to stay in the moment of each day, trying to find the stability I longed for in just the moment that I was in. Nothing more. That was a significant change for me. My career and my nature caused me to typically plan far into the future. I knew all too well, though, that anything can change in a flash of a moment. Pema writes, "Impermanence is the essence of life, but nothing ever goes away until it has taught us what we need to know" (pg. 165). What was I meant to learn from this slowed down, still time of my life?

I wrote in my journal before Thanksgiving 2018 that, "God seems to be getting my attention so as to ready me for what I am meant to do next in my life." I felt God placed me in the center of what Caroline Myss, PhD, describes in *Sacred Contracts, Awakening Your Divine Potential* as "a cluster of disasters in a remarkably short time that reroutes your life." She points out that the word disaster means "from the stars," reflecting our entrenched cultural belief that "terrible things happen for reasons only known by the Heavens" (pg. 81). Yes, terrible losses shadowed my life—losing my son, possibly my marriage, possibly my career. Was there something I needed to learn from all of this loss?

I felt a deep yearning for understanding what I was meant to do now if I learned to live with my son being a spirit, possibly being on my own, and no familiar job ordering my days. What was my purpose for the rest of the time I have on this planet? I no longer feared my death. I saw it now as a portal, hopefully not too uncomfortable, to Heaven, and to my next life. I saw my body aging; I felt my stamina fading and my motivation to keep striving dimming. What was I supposed to do with my time left in my taxed physical body?

I often asked this question of my son: "Ethan, what do I need to know, to do, for the rest of my years on this planet in order to be fulfilling my purpose? You know so much more than I do, now that you are in Heaven. Could you share with me something that would help me?" I asked this question of Ethan mostly when I was outside, running or walking, or just sitting in my garden. But I never heard an answer from Ethan. Was I still too shrouded with grief to hear him speak to me?

I decided to try connecting with him through a new medium, Robynne. She walked back and forth during the reading, listening intently to Ethan's message for me. "He is telling you this: 'Keep healing, Mom. Think of me when you see a hawk; that is me flying above you, watching over you and loving you.'"

Robynne cautioned me to cease trying so hard to reach out to Ethan; she said I must "be still and quiet, let Ethan come to *you*, let him speak to you in symbols, the language of spirits. You are to feel joy when you see a hawk, knowing that Ethan is happy and whole. He has never left you." She said that if I healed, it would "trickle down to Ethan's father, and to his sister." I took this message from Ethan to heart. Okay, then, I decided I would continue learning the things I was meant to learn.

I felt called to return to reading *Sacred Contracts*, which I had started some years prior to Ethan's illness. I never got very far when I first started it, because at that time I didn't have a strong context in which to seriously explore my spiritual journey or truly question if I was off course. I am chagrined to admit that prior to Ethan's death, I had not really contemplated in a serious way what my soul's journey—my spiritual journey—might demand of me now while I was on Earth. I thought I was doing what I was supposed to do here: I tried to live a Christian life, believe in God, and try to help others reconnect with their spiritual selves, whether through my role as a psychotherapist or as a yoga teacher. I deeply believe that the psychological wounds people suffer are often of a spiritual nature as well, and I try to help them heal their spiritual selves, too. It was time to challenge myself to learn what else God was calling me to do on my spiritual journey, my journey that now included being a mother to a son who was with me as a spirit.

So, I did all of the soul-searching exercises Dr. Myss includes in her book to better understand my spiritual potential—my highest purpose—that which would reflect my soul's journey, not just my earthly journey. If I was off course, I wanted to know how to get on course as fast as possible (so typical of me).

Dr. Myss maintains that your "divine potential becomes more audible as you release your need to know why things happen as they do" (pg. 18). Well, surely that was why I wasn't hearing messages about my divine potential! My spiritual ears had been straining for so long to hear the answers to all of my "why" questions! Why did my son develop a deadly addiction and die? Why was my marriage on shaky ground? Why was I coming to the end of a long career? I felt that my life plan had been terribly, even unfairly, disrupted. But Dr. Myss calls this type of experience of one's life being turned upside down a "soul contract intervention." I now viewed the "Dark Mary" oracle card I had been given a month ago at my yoga retreat as a message from God that he was disrupting my life for a purpose. Perhaps I needed to heed this spiritual sign as a message that I needed to be ready to accept more change.

Our "sacred contract" represents the "Earthly commitments, the tasks you have been assigned, and the lessons you agreed to learn in this incarnation on Earth in order to fulfill your divine potential" (pg. 17). What *were* the lessons I agreed to learn while on this planet, during the short time I am in my physical body? Perhaps as part of my soul's contract I was *meant* to be Ethan's mother, partnering with Jeff as his father and Deva as his sister, walking with Ethan on his journey of battling depression and addiction. Perhaps I was *asked* to be a witness to his time on this planet, and *accept* that his time ended before mine. I now had the opportunity to *use* what I was learning to help and heal others who suffer as Ethan did. But I was slowly becoming aware that I also needed to change the way I was caring for myself, change something about the way I was living *my* life.

As I dove back into *Sacred Contracts*, I learned that Dr. Myss organizes one's pathway toward understanding one's divine potential by discovering what mix of twelve archetypes comprises one's personality. Archetypes are neither good nor bad. They are universal manifestations of humanity's way of expressing oneself across time and across cultures. Then, she guides one through understanding how our unique mix of archetypes can help steer us toward making wiser choices. This understanding also helps us avoid behaviors that sabotage our achievement of our highest purpose for the greatest good.

Two of my archetypes that I initially perceived as negative—Thief and Addict—I learned were part of me in order to protect me from engaging in negative harmful behaviors. Dr. Myss states that "everyone of us is touched by the Addict Archetype in some way. In its positive aspect, this archetype helps you recognize when an outside substance, habit, relationship, or any expression of life has more authority over your willpower than does your inner spirit" (pg. 365). I saw that over the course of my life, I had at various times not listened to myself with regard to moderating intense exercise or taking on projects and tasks where I became overcommitted. I thus stole my time from myself and also from nurturing my relationship with God and devoted it instead to earthly pursuits.

After intensive self-examination, I developed my "archetypal wheel" guided by the framework Dr. Myss provides. I determined that my two strongest archetypes are teacher and healer. That confirmed my roles as a psychotherapist, yoga teacher, public speaker, and trainer. What I didn't anticipate is the work I needed to do regarding the four archetypes of survival that she states we all universally have: Child, Saboteur, Victim, and Prostitute. Ah, there was that concept of relating to life as a victim again! I had a growing awareness that at times I felt my life was unfairly happening *to* me, and that I protested some of those events with, "Why me?" which is reflective of a victim stance. I also knew that I was burdened in my life by still carrying some wounds from my childhood, reflective of the Wounded Child archetype, a common subset of the Child archetype. I heeded the core learnings of the Prostitute archetype that told me I needed to enhance my self-esteem and self-respect. My attention was called to situations where I had been at risk of being sabotaged, or sabotaging myself, from actualizing my own power or success.

In addition to these six, I chose six other archetypes that reflected my sacred contract, to total twelve. Dr. Myss then instructs one via a process of a guided meditation to place each archetype within one of the twelve houses of the Zodiac. This was an amazing process that has helped me to face some difficult truths within me. It also helped to confirm my strengths. I am a physically oriented person, so it made sense to me that one of my archetypes was Athlete. That it would fall into the house of Sagittarius, which is the zodiac sign that fuels the inspiration, the devotion, and the passion to develop one's relationship with God, confirmed my awareness that I have deepened my spiritual relationship with God through my yoga practice. Another one of my archetypes was Judge. This would prove to be the one that I would wrestle with most deeply. This would prove to be the archetype that was hindering me from fully actualizing my divine potential.

I sat still after my deep dive into my archetype study. I saw that I needed to challenge the Judge within me in order to be able move toward my soul's purpose. Ethan and all the healers from whom I had sought counsel were right. I was realizing that this changed relationship with myself was not going to be easy. Chagrined, I smiled at myself that here I was at the "late" age of fifty-eight-years-old, and I was challenged with this type of—literal—soul healing! But God's timetable is not necessarily the same as our timetable. My soul sister's mother Marjorie says, "We grow when we grow and we learn when we learn." So, judging myself for having this kind of self-healing to do at this stage of life was not helpful. I tried to follow the voice inside of me—my wisest voice, and the voice of Ethan—that said, "Keep on learning, Robin. Let go of judgement."

Chapter 27
ETHAN IS MY TEACHER

Near the second anniversary of Ethan's death I received a "HealthCare Hero" award from BizTimes, a Milwaukee community organization that honors those who work in health care and contribute in an outstanding way to the health of their community. In receiving my award for fighting the Opioid Epidemic in the Milwaukee area, I referenced one of my archetypes in my acceptance remarks: "I know that God created me to be a Warrior. Ethan, I believe that you and God conspired before you were born for me to be your mom. You somehow knew that I would continue to fight the disease of addiction for others, as I tried to fight it for you. God put you into my life to teach me what I needed to know to help others after you were gone. Thank you, Ethan, for the privilege of being your mother and for all you have taught me."

The dearth of positive memories we have of Ethan in the years as he transitioned from an adolescent boy to an adult man is a sorrow to me. A wonderful memory I do have, however, is of him teaching me a skill, a skill that was all about fun. I treasure this memory as another gift Ethan gave me. After his sophomore year at University of Wisconsin-La Crosse, he came home to live and work for the summer at the City of Greenfield Department of Public Works.

One late afternoon after a grueling hot day outside, he took a dip in our pool, and I joined him when I came home after work. He began jumping off the diving board, showing off for his mom.

After watching him do a few back dives, I said, "You know, I've always wanted to be able to do a back dive, but I don't think I can."

He enthusiastically said, "You can, Mom, I'll show you how right now!" He proceeded to carefully explain the importance of positioning on the diving board.

"It's really key, Mom, that you get up on balls of your feet at the very edge of the board, and let your heels hover over the edge. Now, sit back like you are doing chair pose in yoga—ha, ha, I knew you would get that! Flex your knees, Mom—more—there you go. Now, push off the board with your arms up, and think about arching *up* and then back." Earnestly he added, "I know it is counter-intuitive, Mom, to think of going up in the air before you go backwards into the water, but that part is very important to trust yourself to do, or you will just slap into the water on your back, and that won't feel good, I guarantee it!"

Of course, that is exactly what I did, and for my next several attempts as well. Each time when I came up for air, he was laughing, but kindly said to me, "Are you okay, Mom? Try again, I know you can do this!"

Finally, I was ready to give up, and I said, "Thanks, Ethan, but I think I'm done, I can't seem to get the hang of this!"

Ethan said, "C'mon, Mom, you almost have this. Don't give up now! You need to *trust* your body that if you go up first, and then arch over backwards, that your head *will* enter the water first, not your back. You won't hit the diving board, trust yourself. Feel it, Mom. Trust yourself!"

I smiled to myself as I treaded water in the deep end, listening to his passionate teaching. I thought, "This is interesting being on the receiving end of this coaching and cheerleading from my son, and not the other way around." I got back up on that diving board and repeated his instructions to myself. "Trust yourself Robin. You can do this." And I did. I let go of trying so hard and I felt my way to a beautiful back dive, head first into the water.

I will never forget the look on Ethan's face when I came up for air, pumping my fist. He looked so pleased for me, but also pleased with himself for teaching me something as cool as a back dive. His face was bright with joy and his blue eyes sparkled with the sheer enjoyment of seeing me so gleeful, and with his achievement of teaching me. His voice was full of pride in me and in himself. His dad came home just then from work, and Ethan wanted to show Jeff what he had taught me. This was Ethan at his best—fun, generous, supportive, strong, and self-assured. I believe with my whole heart that part of my soul contract is that I must teach and help others with the same attitude of strength, love, and joy that he showed me that day.

As Christmas of 2018 approached, the two year mark of Ethan's death, I was feeling lighter as I was working on letting go of my self-blame and my anger at God that Ethan had died. I was not letting my energy be siphoned off into asking "why" questions as much. I went for a run on a sunny, chilly Saturday morning along the Menomonee River in Wauwatosa. I talked to Ethan as I often did when I ran. We had enjoyed tossing words back and forth to each other with a random theme when he was alive, so as I was running on the path along the river, I chose alliteration as the theme for my word play with Ethan that morning.

I said out loud, "The river is beautiful this morning, Ethan. It's a babbling brook, no, burbling…hmmm, maybe even bubbling along. It's barreling along, bumbling over rocks, and bumping up against logs." I laughed, thinking he could come up with better words than those. I said, "Do you see how it is flowing along so lovely, Ethan? How would *you* describe it? You can only choose words starting with a 'b.'"

I stopped running and let myself look around at the sunshine twinkling on the rushing water, the translucent clouds of my breath in the crisp air, the white frost sparkling on all of the branches and grasses on the river's edge. Suddenly, I realized I felt happy! At that moment, the word "breathtaking" popped into my mind. Ethan's answer.

I smiled and said, "Good word, Ethan. It's perfect." I started running again, but after a few more strides, I inexplicably slowed and then stopped again. It was unheard of for me to stop so close to finishing a run. But I wanted to prolong the sweetness of the rare contentment I was feeling. I breathed deeply in the beauty of the morning and my place in it. What a gift for me to be in this moment having this conversation with Ethan like we used to!

It was then that I felt Ethan. I saw and felt at the same time a clear entity of pure crystal energy to my left as I lifted my face up to him, smiling. Ethan felt palpable to me. He was real, but effervescent, too. He stayed there for a second, oh, long sweet second, and then softly, gently evaporated. I stood stock still for a few breaths, and then moved down the path as it widened into a field. As I walked, I felt a strong prolonged prickling across my upper back toward my left shoulder. It felt wonderful. I felt the prickling cup my left shoulder and upper arm. I recognized immediately the embrace of my son. He always slung his left arm around people's shoulders. "I love you, too, Ethan!" I said as we walked together for a few breaths. Then he was gone. I didn't feel sad. I felt peaceful and full of love. I felt hopeful he would be back again sometime. I was finally able to receive his spirit's presence in my life.

After that day, I began to be more open to Ethan teaching me how to relate to him as my spirit son. Accepting the message that I deserved to enjoy moments of happiness and contentment. Believing that the boundary between him and me is but a breath. Growing trust in the reality of my spirit son who I cannot see, physically touch, or hear speak. There were some days, though, that I doubted that I could maintain that trust.

God lovingly chided me, saying, "My daughter, you already have a map for how to have trust in that which you cannot see. I gave you that map in My relationship with you and all of My children."

I replied, "I know, God, but I wasn't around when You were alive in Your physical body. I didn't experience You in the flesh and blood and then have You taken away from me like my son was taken from me!"

When I argue with God like this, I sometimes hear Ethan's voice that summer day of my back dive triumph telling me to, "Trust, and just feel it, Mom!"

Chapter 28

LETTING GO

Something that Ethan couldn't teach me was the shift I had to make within myself before I could have a relationship with him as a spirit son. I had to completely let go of the fierce mothering of my son that I did for so long before he died: my efforting to motivate him to stay in treatment, my searching ceaselessly for new strategies or treatments that might help him, setting boundaries with him that were agonizing but critical to protect Jeff and me from the pain of repeatedly broken trust. Holding on to the fear of losing him, dreading that possible outcome daily for years, till it became our norm. Holding on to those strong emotions had drained me and strained my marriage almost beyond repair. I had to let go of all of that in order to open myself up to trusting—believing—that Ethan was well, happy, and safely surrounded by God and His angels. I was still stuck for a long time after his death in relating to him as my young-adult ill son, caged in his body and mind from his addiction. I listened to voicemails I'd saved of his voice over and over again; I looked for long moments at the dozens of photos of him I had plastered on our refrigerator; I touched his clothing, slept in his bed. I hated to relinquish him as my flesh and blood son.

One Sunday morning, mid-January 2019 with Christmas and the two year anniversary of Ethan's death behind us, I sat in my sunny living room having my morning coffee. I rested my gaze across the room upon the cedar chest next to the fireplace, as I had done hundreds of times in the last two years. It was still covered with the mementos, framed photos, and artifacts of Ethan's life that I had gathered for his funeral display two years earlier. A large filigree gold basket given to me by my daughter's mother-in-law still held all of the sympathy cards we received. Hundreds of loving, kind, supportive words were held in that basket. Words are a great source of comfort to me, and just looking at that basket lifted me up for two years. Just as seeing the evidence in the mementos that Ethan *had* been a boy, a teenager, a man, was a comfort to me.

The morning sun, low in the winter sky, shone in through the south-facing window and illuminated a 5x7 photo of Ethan's face on the cedar chest. It was an amazing head shot of him, grinning from ear to ear, taken with Ariana on top of Granddad's Bluff in La Crosse. We had used it as his obituary photo. The sun beamed across and lit up his face so brightly that he seemed to come alive. His face was bathed in clear golden light. I stared at him, transfixed. He was shining and smiling at me. I felt lightness and peace, soft as gossamer strands, wrap around my heart as I continued to gaze at him. I said, "Yes, I see you, Ethan. You are light now, pure golden light! You look so happy." It took six minutes for the sun to continue on its way across the sky and then the photo returned to simply being the photographic image of Ethan. I felt that Ethan was telling me that it was okay to dismantle the shrine I had maintained from the funeral for two years, because he was not there in those physical things, but rather was alive in my heart.

So, that is what we did. I checked with Jeff, and he said, "I knew you would know when it was time; I'm ready, too." Deva came over and we together gently and respectfully dismantled this display of Ethan's life. The empty cedar chest looked forlorn, so we removed that too, and placed an antique church pew in its place that I had refinished years ago. I suddenly felt scared I would forget how

Ethan looked if all the photos were gone. Jeff said, "We can always put it all back if we need to." At Deva's wise suggestion, I tucked some of the photos into corners around the house, so that evidence of him was still with us.

I loved seeing a visual image of my sweet son, but as time went on, I found I needed less and less evidence of his former physical self surrounding me. In my mind's eye, I saw him more and more as a shining young man filled with pure light and dissolving into pure love.

In the GRASP group I facilitate, I encourage all attendees to consider completing a therapeutic letter-writing exercise when they are ready. These letters can be shared with the group or kept private. The first letter is a letter to your loved one, saying all of the things left in your heart, words unspoken due to the wrenching suddenness of death by drug overdose. Then, when you are ready, the second letter is a reply to yourself written *in the voice* and *from the heart* of your loved one. Our group has found much healing in this exercise.

I wrote my letter to Ethan eighteen months after he died and read it to the group. Jeff shared his letter as well. After the second anniversary of Ethan's death, I was on a winter run and suddenly Ethan was communicating his reply to me as I ran on the snowy, quiet parkway at twilight. This was the same parkway Jeff had found him almost dead at age eighteen. As soon as I got home, I stood at the kitchen counter, growing chilled in my sweaty running gear as I wrote it all down just as I heard him speak to me.

Dear Ma—ok, Dear MOM, I know you hate the word "Ma" (it was then that I knew it was Ethan; this is exactly how he would start out),

You weren't ready until now to get this letter from me. But I see that you have done the work to understand that you have a sacred contract to fulfill while you are on Earth in your physical body. Just as I did.

I chose you as my mom because I knew you would have the strength, courage, and stamina to be my mom through my life, but especially during the long years I battled my depression, anxiety, and drug abuse. You are a teacher, healer, and a warrior. You have the qualities to help other parents through the grief of losing a child to addiction. You are a warrior in this opioid epidemic.

But you are not alone, Mom. There are warriors all over this country. I know, because there are many souls here in the spirit world with me who chose their parents for the same reason I chose you and Dad.

The opioid epidemic will lessen in your lifetime, but addiction will remain tenacious in its vicious hold on people for a long, long time. You are to continue to fight against the stigma and the shame associated with addiction. That is your piece of the fight, Mom. Others will address the brain chemistry piece and teach people how to heal from addiction or avoid it completely. Many of us had to succumb to this epidemic in order for this healing work to be generated.

I know you can do this, Mom. But you aren't meant to do it alone. Let others help you. That will be hard for you. I was like you, Mom. It was hard for me to let in the help of others. Be open to help. Be vulnerable.

Mom, every morning during the visits I had at home during my college years and after, you would wake me up in the morning and badger me to, "Get up, Ethan! Let's go for a walk, Ethan! Let's go get breakfast, Ethan! Let's talk, Ethan—what do you want to talk about?" I acted like I was irritated, but I loved those invitations. As do other people love to be invited! So—invite them to walk with you. Talk with others. Listen to them. Get breakfast with them. Figure this out. You love to figure things out, Mom. Speak up while you are figuring it out. Speak up loud, Mom.

Remember, you are not alone in this fight.
I love you so much. I am so thankful for what you did to help me and
that you loved me through it all.
Your son forever,
Ethan

I shared this letter from my son at my next GRASP group meeting. When I read it aloud, it struck me that my son's reminder that I did not need to journey alone was the same message I had written in my letter to *him* the night before he died. My burgeoning awareness that I was on a spiritual journey that I could not turn my back on was confirmed by Ethan's letter to me. But. But. But—I felt like Jonah from the Bible who tried to avoid the hard task God asked him to do. Jonah's disobedience of God landed him in the belly of a whale. I didn't sign up for this heavy responsibility when Jeff and I decided to have a second child!

During the months I had been on medical leave, I reread all of my journals from college to try to glean more knowledge about my sacred contract. Maybe my younger self was wiser than my older broken self. I was touched by one entry from my sophomore year—how young I was!—in which I inexplicably wrote, "I am looking forward to being a mother someday." This was a strange statement for me to make, as I never really liked kids that much. I didn't enjoy babysitting as a teenager, I found kids to be slightly irritating. However, after I married Jeff and completed my Master's degree, we wanted to start a family. I discovered that I loved being a mother.

If I would have known as a young woman that part of my sacred contract would be to learn to be a mother to a spirit son, I would have said to God, "No, I can't do that. I don't want to do that! I don't know how. Please, God, don't give me that sorrow."

But God does what God knows is best for our greatest good and highest purpose. Perhaps it is not that God gives us sorrows. Sorrow may simply but miserably be part of what happens to us because we live in a broken world. We bring that on ourselves living in the fallen world we live in. Perhaps it is that God arranges for the most good to come out of our sorrows. Perhaps my enthusiastic younger self had the right attitude—being a mother is a privilege. My older self tries every day to accept, even celebrate, that I was chosen for this contract of being Ethan's mother, even while struggling to make sense of the sorrowful parts.

Through my struggling, I *was* changing. One of my Siesta Key soul sisters sent me this note after spending an evening with me and another friend who has walked my journey with me:

Robin, something about you last night came through…I can't quite name it…a sort of calm in your eyes, like the very worst of the pain is moving through, like you've begun to trust that there is a certain level of healing from the stunning loss you're enduring every day. Even with all of the pain, there is a grace in your eyes, less fight, less writhe, something calmer and more open and accepting. It's beautiful on you, Robin.

Another of my soul sisters also noticed a change in me. JeMae was caught off guard during a weekend Jeff and I were visiting her and her family mid-February. I started joking around and teasing her and her daughter Jenny. The first time I did that, she and Jenny stared at me, silent.

I looked at them and asked, "Hey, what's wrong?"

JeMae said wonderingly, "I can't believe it. You are joking around again with me. I haven't seen that in you since Ethan died." She gave me a big hug and they both finally laughed with me.

By March 1st, 2019, I had decided to resign from my job as a Director of Outpatient Behavioral Health Services. After five months of medical leave, my PTSD had not improved enough for me to return to the environment at my workplace. I had to let go of my career with that organization. It was another loss. A loss of my professional identity, my professional relationships, and a source of self-worth. I tried to see this ending as an opportunity to reinvent myself after more than a decade in leadership roles.

After resigning, delightful opportunities for traveling came my way. Jeff and I planned our first family vacation with our daughter since Ethan died, to California (the tarot card reader was right!) to visit my nephew, who is like a son to me, and his girlfriend. Also, two of my soul sisters and I planned a "girls getaway" to Siesta Key, Florida, where one of them has a condo right on the ocean. I was looking forward to these spring trips and felt some hopefulness that a fresh start lay ahead for me. Maybe my friend was right, that the very worst of the pain *had* passed. If she saw this change in me, maybe my life finally was moving into a more hopeful stage.

I didn't know that two weeks later I would be in the middle of a firestorm of such searing hurt and betrayal that I would be laid down so low that I didn't care if I lived or died. I was not in the final stage of change in my grief journey. I was like Jonah, still in the dark belly of the whale. But I was unlike Jonah in that I wasn't able to surrender into praising God while disasters continued to fall like limbs from trees in a thunderstorm around me.

Chapter 29
RADICAL ACCEPTANCE

Transformational change can feel like chaos. In the chaos in which I was drowning, I was stripped down to my most essential self as I was forced to accept the reality of another loss—the loss of my marriage. I discovered that my husband had not ended his emotional affair as he had promised.

I asked him to leave. I couldn't breathe, I couldn't think straight, I didn't know what to do. I felt as though I was back in the black sea of grief. This was a disaster of cruel proportions. I sat up for most of the night, praying alternately for God to help me survive and to strike down my husband.

I spent the next three weeks in shock. Forty-eight hours after I learned that Jeff's affair was ongoing, Deva and I went alone on our "family" trip to Santa Ana, California. We spent a sunny week with my nephew and his girlfriend, hosted in his aunt and uncle's beautiful, calm, serene home. I tried each day to stay focused on them and enjoy the precious time with them, but I don't think I was very successful. I did my best to be a supportive aunt, but I was a shadow of my best self. The progress I had made in uncovering her seemed lost.

Ten days after returning home from California, I departed for my next trip to Siesta Key. What a treat for someone who lives in gray and cold Wisconsin to escape to the beach in late winter. I could let go and just be. My soul sisters on the beach listened to me, loved me, and gave me space to just mourn. They sat shiva with me while I mourned the loss of my trust in my husband, while I mourned the hope I had tentatively allowed into my heart after I decided not to return to work and to take a year off and reinvent myself. In order to mourn those losses, I needed patient witnesses sitting with me.

We sat on the beach for five days, talking, crying, laughing. I listened to the waves giving up and losing their shape on the shore ceaselessly…I listened to the wind sighing, the seagulls wailing and crying…I listened to the sound of the sun on the beach. Did you know that the sun has a sound when it is shining down on you when you are sitting in loss? It sounds like OM, the quiet hum of all creation. It is a sound that softly permeates you with warmth, wrapping around you with steady presence. I heard the faint sounds of laughter and chatty voices of other people on the beach. I looked enviously at people walking past our lounge chairs, seemingly care-free. I so longed to feel carefree. Sitting on my beach chair with sisters and sunshine wrapping themselves around me, I was at least surviving.

As soon as I returned home to our empty house, nothing felt safe. What I thought I could trust about my husband, I was wrong. Who I thought my husband was, he was not. How could he have lived this double life? What I thought was my life with a partner of thirty-four years was apparently not. Where was the hopeful-ness of a fresh start that we had just spoken of a few weeks ago when we moved my belongings out of my work office on a Saturday morning? We had a celebratory beer at a local brewery. We clinked glasses, and Jeff toasted to, "A new beginning, Robin, for you."

I didn't know how to accept this reality, to live with this real-ity. I ruminated on what had gone so terribly wrong…had I taken too long to heal after our son's death? Were we too far apart in our grief to ever find our way back to each other? Was the stress of my being on medical leave for five months too great? I sank deeper in my confusion and pain. I felt like I had been kicked to the curb, disposed of, just when I had taken the courageous step of leaving my job. Two days after returning from sunny Siesta Key, I fell onto my knees on my living room floor, tipped over, and couldn't move. I lay there face down on the carpeting and just wished I was done. Just done. I didn't want to *make* my life be done, I just wanted to be whisked away out of this morass of hurt. I suddenly knew—I don't know how I knew this—I just knew, that I needed to go somewhere safe, somewhere else. I needed an emotional ICU *right now*. I needed to be gathered up by someone who could tell me what to do, how to be, how to cope. I had reached the end of my ability to be in the chaos alone.

If I win a lottery, or find a pot of gold at the end of a rainbow, I will create a franchise of Emotional ICUs all across the country and staff them with angels who will care for those of us whose hearts are broken and souls have been sliced apart. Since that doesn't exist anywhere that I know of now, I called a psychiatric hospital instead. Within two hours, my daughter was sitting beside me as I was admitted to an adult inpatient psychiatric unit. I hadn't eaten for a day and a half, so the soft spoken nurse "rustled up a bit of lunch" and set it in front of me. I stared at it on the tray. It was the tray that made me realize I really was in a hospital. I was escorted to my room. I would be sharing a room with a sleeping young woman who didn't stir as I sat on my bed and placed my hand on my crunchy plastic pillow. I put the paper bag with my extra shirt, yoga pants, lip balm, my daily devotion book, my journal, and my reading glasses beside me on the floor next to my bed. No shoes, no toiletries, no access to food or drink when I want it, no cell phone, no door on the bathroom. Less stuff means less decisions to make on a daily basis. No one and nothing to take care of. What a blessing. It occurred to me much later when I reflected on that moment that this is what Jeff had expressed to me he wanted nine months earlier. I exhaled deeply and lay down.

A judgmental voice began rippling through my head: "What have I done, putting myself here? I am a psychotherapist; I should know how to care for myself in this type of situation, dire as it is…I have helped others through trauma and loss and pain, why couldn't I shepherd myself through my shit without taking myself to a hospital? What is wrong with me?"

My journal entry that evening, written in a felt tip marker because pens weren't allowed on the unit, said, "I have been stripped down to nothing but myself. Perhaps that is where I need to start. Perhaps that is not nothing, but everything I need to find a way forward. Let go of everything you know as a therapist, Robin. Just be a person. Let it all go. Radically accept where you are, Robin. Not just physically where you are, but where you are in your life."

So, I did. I followed the routines of the morning goal-setting group and set a daily goal for myself. I attended the experiential therapy group, rolling my eyes internally, thinking, "I am so *not* going to do an art project," until I became absorbed in that very assignment. With colored pencils I drew a picture of myself being tumbled about inside a tidal wave of many blue colors tipped with frothy white foam. The wave wasn't trying to destroy me; the wave looked like it was lifting me up to deposit me on the warm sandy beach dotted with green palms. Kind of like the ocean does over and over again for Moana in the Disney movie of the same name.

I attended everything the unit offered. I went to the CBT skills group, the mindfulness group, the DBT skills group; I tried the dual diagnosis group because I was worried that I had been relying on wine to help me cope. At first, I had to force myself to interact with others on the unit during meals and social times, but quickly I found it interesting to hear about what brought others to the unit. I refrained from offering any advice. I was just another wounded person like everyone else. I attended every meal and was grateful that I had good, healthy food to eat that I didn't need to prepare for myself. I attended the evening "wrap-up" group in which we processed together what we had learned and accomplished during the day. We complimented each other, high-fiving at times.

I was impressed by the courageous work I saw others doing. I was touched by the kindnesses I saw occur all around me: the patients supporting each other in the rawest of conversations, the nurses being unfailingly patient and helpful, the group therapists being easygoing but effective in teaching critical skills that we all needed to learn. Or, in some cases, to remember to use them. We were reassured that these skills *would* often work if we would use them regularly. I was surprisingly thankful for the experience at the end of the four days I spent there. While I didn't learn anything I didn't already cognitively know, I did experience the psychological healing benefit of letting others care for me.

I was referred to a half day aftercare program called the Intensive Outpatient Program (IOP), which I agreed to attend. Why not? I was open to anything God was sending my way. But being back home even a half day, I got stuck, again, in asking "why" questions of God. Why am I on the receiving end of such hurtful betrayal—not once, but now *twice* from my husband? If he was so unhappy, why couldn't he just have spoken up and honestly told me how he felt? Why is this happening to me? I was thinking like a victim again.

Back at home, I was consumed by anger so harsh that I stripped all of the photos of him in our home, I took all of his things and bagged and boxed them up in the basement so I didn't see any trace of him in our home where I was living alone. While in the basement, I came upon a box of our school yearbooks and our love letters we had exchanged in the early years of our relationship and marriage. I didn't remember saving them, but I surely was going to throw them out now! Breathing heavily with tears in my eyes, I started to heave the heavy box up into my arms—wanting to both embrace the box and throw it against the wall. The box shifted against the left side of my body, and as my left arm jerked to grab the box from falling, I felt a snap at the top of my left shoulder, and within minutes I couldn't use my left arm. I ended up needing surgery immediately to repair my torn left bicep.

The surgery interrupted my IOP attendance for a week. Planning for how I was to manage my recovery post-surgery was daunting. It became clear to me very quickly how vulnerable I was living alone for the first time in my life. I had no partner to rely on to transport me to and from surgery, to help me once I was home getting settled on the couch, to keep my icing machine on my shoulder replenished with ice, help me prepare meals, to help me get to the bathroom, to help me get in and out of bed, to help me walk and feed Roxy. I had to reassure myself that it was okay to be dependent on others. I assembled a list of no less than nine women who helped me those first two weeks: my daughter, my niece, dear friends, even a friend who drove from Minnesota for a weekend to plant my spring pots up for me, women from my GRASP group, my neighbor. I joked with my daughter that "You are so sweet to come straight from your long day at work to tuck me into bed; you probably owe me at least several thousand bed-tuckings!"

I was showered with love, support, and companionship. I let myself be rained down upon. I put aside my pride and asked a friend to help me change my clothes, help me shower, help me change my bandage. I accepted their love gracefully and loved them back. Victor Hugo wrote in *Les Miserables*, "To love another person you see the face of God." God was showing me his face over and over again in my post-surgery helpers.

I returned to IOP and spent five weeks there, learning—relearning, because I already knew it—Dialectical Behavioral Therapy (DBT) skills. I had to figure out how to live with realities in my life that were painful. I had to surrender my "why" questions and discover how I would move forward with my life the way it was, not the way I wanted it to be. Here is where I came face to face with one of my hardest life lessons: radical acceptance. Profoundly and deeply accepting something As. It. Is. Period. Not fighting against the reality. I'm a fighter, but fighting against some things in my life was harming me.

My son had an addiction and died from it. I cannot change that reality. My workplace culture was the way it was. I cannot change that. My husband had broken our marriage vows. I cannot change that. Being immersed for three hours each day in DBT philosophy, I had the support and courage to radically accept the painful events that had occurred in my life.

One day after IOP, I felt the question surfacing in my heart that Jeff had asked me a few months after Ethan died. He and I were working on rebuilding trust after he ended his emotional affair the first time. He had asked me, "Do you want to know why I talked to her?" I did *not* want to know his answers to that question. We never discussed it. But on some level, I knew.

A deep awareness was now bubbling to the surface in me. All of the work I was doing was propelling me to look deep within myself in a new way. I had examined and was radically accepting my mothering of Ethan as being the best I could do. I had examined and then radically accepted my decision to leave my job. I thought, then, I was stripped down to my essential self. But not quite. I needed to face the reality that I wasn't the wife to Jeff that I thought I was. I saw that I had abandoned Jeff in my own way after Ethan died. I didn't intend to do that. But I was so lost in my grief that I couldn't be there for him. My soul sister from Siesta Key told me a story of Jeff coming to her house, and sharing with her husband his feelings that, "A part of me is relieved that Ethan died; I couldn't have continued coping with his relapses…It was too hard. I can never say this to Robin. She wouldn't understand. She told me she could have gone on forever supporting Ethan." He was right. I wouldn't have accepted those feelings of Jeff's. My judgment of Jeff's grief as unacceptable was a way that I had failed him.

I also had to face the reality that I had given sparse support to Jeff in his efforts to build a post-retirement career after 2014. Our Christmas card the year of 2014 celebrated Jeff retiring as a police detective, Deva graduating with a master's degree in social work, and Ethan graduating from college with a major in psychology and a minor in criminal justice. During those years between 2014 and 2016, before Ethan died, Jeff was trying to build a new career at the same time that Deva was trying to establish herself in her career and Ethan was declining. I wasn't expansive enough. I wasn't big-hearted enough. My bandwidth was not wide enough. Ethan got the best of me, my work and my daughter got the second best of me, and my marriage got the least of me.

What happens when we do harm that we don't intend? What do we do with our failures when we see with new eyes the impact that they have on the ones we love? How do we accept our imperfections and forgive ourselves for the harm we do to the ones we love most?

A thought suddenly struck me. The place I now found myself was not unlike the Twelve-Step work of a person recovering from addiction. I had to radically accept that I was powerless over others' choices—that of my husband and my son. This is similar to Step One. I had to humbly account within myself for how I had harmed my husband and take ownership for that. This is similar to Steps Four, Nine, and Ten.

I remembered discovering in Ethan's Residential Treatment Journal the pages and pages of work he had done on a complete accounting of the effects of his drug use on himself and others, and the plans he had for making amends. In reading his handwritten words, I was impressed by his raw honesty and the insight he displayed in doing this Step work. His courage in doing that hard work inspired me now.

I have come to recognize that Ethan's spirit communicates with me to help me, when thoughts about him come to me seemingly from nowhere. They are coming from somewhere. They are coming from my son to me. I listened.

I decided I needed to make some amends to my husband. Now, not later. I had to take responsibility of the ways I had abandoned him, not only focus on the ways I felt victimized and harmed by him. So, I wrote a long letter to my husband. I described to Jeff the ways that I felt I let him down, abandoned him, was unloving toward him during the years before Ethan died and in our separate grief journeys since then. I took responsibility for the ways I had let him down. I asked him to forgive me. I then implemented radical forgiveness and tried very hard to transform my anger towards him into forgiveness. I prayed to God to help me with this difficult work. Jeff deserved it, and I deserved to do this work for me as well.

I also decided to begin to behave as though I was a woman who was worthy of being loved, cherished, and valued for what I brought to this world. I needed to befriend my Victim archetype and heed its advice for me: to be aware when I was interacting with my circumstances from a victim stance. I decided to consult an attorney. Though we had been living apart for three months already, I filed for legal separation. Jeff and I met to discuss how we could communicate effectively around finances, house maintenance, and house repairs while separated. It felt so sad to be interacting with my husband around these topics, but I needed to establish this boundary.

I realize now without the event of Jeff's betrayal that I may not have pursued the hard examination of myself, and the subsequent humbling admission of my abandonment of my husband. I read somewhere that true forgiveness is when you can thank the person for that experience. So hard to do. I believe that this is one of my life lessons—to embrace my life experiences from a place of curiosity and acceptance for what they have to teach me. I have to embrace Jeff's presence in my life from a place of gratitude for what he has to teach me.

Chapter 30
RETRIEVING MY SOUL

I believe that my chakra energy system had been shocked out of balance after Ethan died. I remained out of balance afterward when I became absorbed with so many activities, trying to distract myself from grief. During the months I was taking time off from work, I had felt myself slowly coming back into balance. That balance was gone. My heart chakra had been compromised due to my vindictive desire to have Jeff hurt as I had hurt. My anger toward my husband had actually resulted in me injuring my own body. The seat of my personal power, my solar plexus or manipura chakra, was weakened. My sacral chakra, the energy needed to move forward, transform, and change, was also compromised. I considered visiting a shaman by the name of Rick for chakra healing. I had heard him and his wife speak at the "Helping Parents Heal" conference a year earlier. I recalled that Rick had been doing this healing work for over twenty years. He had trained to be a spiritual healer after a terrible car accident in which he and his wife Beth survived, but their two children did not.

A shaman is a healer who interacts with the spirit world to channel spirit energies for healing. I contacted Rick who lived about ninety minutes away from me and scheduled a shamanic healing appointment with Rick. I drove to their house, with my pup Roxy along for company, on a stormy evening in late May. I didn't have any idea what to expect. I parked in front of a beautiful, large house on top of a knoll in the countryside. I was warmly welcomed by this couple. They showed me photos of their deceased children, and the three children they had after their loss. Rick frankly looked like a construction foreman, burly in a teddy-bearish sort of way, dressed in jeans, a plain blue t-shirt, and athletic shoes. No flowing robes, long hair, or sandals. The minute he led me to his healing space on the third floor of their home and began talking with me, I sensed a deep calm, and a very centered presence about him. He asked me why I was seeking to be healed. I said that I had suffered many losses in the past two and a half years—my son, my job, my physical health, and now possibly my marriage.

He asked me to choose a stone from a nearby table. There were many to choose from of different sizes and colors. I am typically drawn to rose quartz, as my favorite color is pink. But, almost outside of my own volition, I found myself choosing a plum-sized black, glossy stone. It felt unusually heavy in my hand. He took it from me and invited me to lie down on what looked like a massage table. I felt very comfortable and not afraid at all. He placed the stone on my belly, my sacral chakra, and said that he was going to begin the healing. He invited me to close my eyes, relax, and breathe.

He did not speak to me for the next forty-five minutes or so. He silently moved about the table I was lying on, sometimes sitting behind my head lightly touching my crown chakra, the top of my head, with his hands. I could hear wind and rain pouring down on the skylights of his third-story healing room. I felt like I was swimming underwater. I felt safe within it, looking upward at the surface where the light was. I wasn't impatient to get to the surface. I felt I was simply waiting for the right time.

In what seemed like just a few breaths, it was over. Rick invited me to sit across from him with a coffee table between us. He said he would describe the healing that he had just done, and I could ask any questions I liked. He began, "The stone you chose was a male meteorite. This stone is not of this world, it has very strong energy which suits you. Your second chakra—the energy center concerned with positive relationships, intimacy, your ability to birth ideas, to be influential—was traumatized and needed healing. Thus, I placed the stone you chose on your belly, your sacral chakra center. But I quickly saw that a part of your soul was missing, so I asked my guides if I needed to do a 'soul retrieval' for you."

He told me that immediately after asking that question he was "pulled down deep into your soul." He found my missing soul piece standing "like a warrior—energetically and determinedly" on a large, smooth, elevated rock, waiting a bit impatiently to be retrieved (so like me). He said my energy was "very strong, but had been unraveled."

He said my energy had been unraveled in my heart due to the loss of trust in my husband, in my mind due to the loss of my identity in my job, in my spirit due to the loss of my child and my faith in God weakened, and my body due to injuring my shoulder and not feeding myself enough. He emphasized, "I found this statement written on the large rock where your soul piece was waiting, Robin, to be retrieved: *You are being unraveled so as to be remade into what you are to become.*" He called this my "soul retrieval contract."

On the journey back from that deep place, Rick told me I was given three gifts. First, my missing soul piece was retrieved, and thus my second chakra was healed. My second gift was that my soul piece was accompanied by my power animal. Rick said he knew immediately when I walked into his room what my power animal was because he observed a horse standing quietly in a corner of the room at the start of the healing. The third gift was a beautiful golden sunrise he saw shining with light and healing energy over me. A sunrise that is similar to the logo of Ethan's Run Against Addiction. This synchronicity was not a surprise to me. He also said, "I sensed angry tearing in your body's energy in your left shoulder, and I closed that negative energetic wound as well."

He said he felt "excitement" for me as he thought about how I was going to knit myself back together again. He told me that I am accompanied on my journey by three spirit guides. He said, "The four of you have been traveling together for many lifetimes. One of you takes a turn rotating into a physical body and the other three accompany the spirit while it is in that body."

I asked, "Who are these three spirits you say I travel with?"

Rick said, "One of them is your son. He seems to be waiting with great patience and expectation for what you are going to become. You seem to be meant to help, heal, and be a voice for others. You have great strength and energy. Do not be afraid."

I literally tried to deeply breathe this message in, so when I lost track of it—and that was sure to happen when I would doubt myself—I could breathe in and remember. I asked who the other two guides are.

He said, "I don't know who the other two are."

I guessed that one of them might be my paternal grandmother, Nana, who had shown herself to me the very first time I met with a medium. I suppose I will find out for sure one day when I am no longer traveling in my physical body.

This healing experience confirmed what I had learned in my sacred contract work: that one of my archetypes is a Warrior and that I have that strength within me to rely upon in following my life's purpose. It also reminded me of a message from Jake, a medium I had consulted six months earlier. I was sad to hear Jake observe that my sense of myself as being a "worthy" person was eroded. Jake told me to keep on doing my healing work. He said, "As you heal, you will meet the 'new Robin,' and you may like her more than the old Robin!" I had more healing work to do.

Rick encouraged me to dialogue with my power animal around what it had to teach me or give to me. He said to spend time around horses if I could, watch movies about horses, read about horses, soak in whatever I could learn from horses. I thought it ironic that my homework was to obsess about horses like the horse-crazy pre-teen girl I had once been. When I told my friend JeMae about my assignment, she tongue-in-cheek mailed me a small stuffed horse to hold. I laughed at myself—here I was, a highly trained mental health professional, tasked with learning from a horse.

Not one to turn away from any opportunity for learning, I discovered that having a horse as one's power animal imparts great strength. Yet its strength regarding its relationship to humans lies in its ability to *submit* to humans, to *serve* them well, and be *in relationship* to them. Likewise, on my journey I discovered strength within myself when I have been most vulnerable with others. In my recent vulnerability, I had found grace coming my way, flowing over me like I had not felt in my life before. Beautiful grace in unexpected, unmerited, sometimes painful gifts that God sent me through my husband, my daughter, my friends, even strangers in my life.

I learned that horse power clears obstacles when you call upon it in specific situations. It can also warn of potential dangers. It has nobility and stamina. Previous to Ethan's death, I had always thought of myself as a strong, even powerful, woman. Why did I need such a strong power animal? But after my shamanic healing experience, I deeply reflected about the quality of my personal power since Ethan died. Who am I? What is my worth? What do I have to offer that is of value? My ability to define myself had grown weaker. I noticed as time went on that my ability to protect myself was diminishing as well. So, connecting with horse power reminded me to access strength, service, and vulnerability.

I remembered when trying to understand why I had a Thief

archetype as part of my sacred contract (that was hard to swallow), I recalled Dr. Myss maintaining that, "The Thief archetype symbolically can take many forms…this archetype prods you to learn to generate power from within," (pg. 418, my emphasis). My Thief archetype fell within Aquarius, the eleventh house in the zodiac, which is focused on one's relationship to the world. Upon more reflection, I recognized that for many years of my adulthood, I felt my personal power was almost solely derived from the roles I inhabited that defined my relationship to the world around me—mother, wife, psychotherapist, yoga teacher, leader at work, in my community, in my church. As some of these roles were being shed from my life, I felt bereft of power.

I realized that another of my life lessons was to find my personal power from within myself, simply from *being* me, not *doing* me. This insight was a significant gift from the shamanic healing. It was also sobering, in that, with this insight came a call to change something in my relationship with myself. I again slid toward self-judgement as I felt I had not internalized what I know to be true about my relationship with God. I know that He loves me simply for being me, not for what I do, or how well I perform. Yet I didn't seem to love myself in that same way.

"Our wounds are often the openings into the best
and most beautiful parts of us."
- David Richo, PhD

Two days after my shamanic healing, I found myself crying like I hadn't done since Ethan died. My tears rolled and dripped down my face. I wiped them away and more came. This flood of grief happened in my therapist's office, a place I feel safe, and where I can say and feel anything. This was a profound contrast to the years before Ethan's death when I rarely cried because it was hard for me to allow myself to be that vulnerable. During those years I felt as though if I cried one tear, a river of tears would pour out of me. Now, I gave myself permission to let that river flow.

I recalled Rick telling me before I left his home that I would either feel tired and sad or energized in the days to follow. Our souls can break apart in response to severe loss or trauma. He warned me that a missing soul piece, when retrieved, brings back with it all of the sadness and grief that it was holding when it broke apart. I felt that to be the case for my soul. I had felt my soul cracking and breaking apart from all of the waves of loss I had experienced in the last two and a half years. I was finally able to let some of that grief run out of me in Josh's office. It felt wonderful to let that grief go. Grief is stored within us in many layers, to be sure. I found it took me many different healing experiences to excavate all of those layers. God must have known that about me, because he sent so many healers my way.

After the catharsis of that healing, I felt myself in the ensuing weeks feeling I was knitting myself back together. I gradually felt more resilient. I felt more whole. I felt relationships shift in my life. I made three new friends as my soul's healing grounded me and gradually integrated me back into my spirit. I had known these women as acquaintances, but after this healing I opened up to developing mutually nurturing friendships with them. Two of them had approached me, to my surprise. These were strong, whole women. According to Chakra energy philosophy, when a person is fragmented, they energetically attract fragmented people. As we become whole, we attract wholeness.

I also felt better able to navigate a separation from Jeff. As I felt less anger toward him, I asked him to consider crafting together our own separation, rather than having expensive attorneys do it for us. He agreed, and so we began discussing what a non-legal separation might look like. We tried our best to interact together positively in front of our daughter Deva, our friends and family to facilitate the second Ethan's Run Against Addiction on June 8th, 2019. When it came to Ethan, we always have been a team. We were able to celebrate this second coming together of over eight hundred runners and walkers who were also fighting against the stigma of addiction and wanting to raise funds for treatment. Threaded through this celebration, however, was deep sadness that Ethan was looking down and seeing his parents so estranged and Deva experiencing her parents so broken.

Chapter 31

MEADOW OF NON-JUDGMENT AND MERCY

After learning from my Victim and Thief archetypes, I knew I needed to finally confront my Judge archetype. I did a brainspotting session with Josh in which I focused on my deep-seated judgment of myself, something that I have carried within me my whole life. I felt such tender sorrow toward myself for carrying that burden so long. In the beginning of my grief journey, I thought I needed to forgive myself, but I knew now that when it came to my relationship with Ethan, I had nothing to forgive myself for. What need was there to forgive myself when I did the very best I could do in being his mother? I saw now that what I needed to do was release my judgmental relationship with myself. I visualized me being a different woman with a different relationship with herself. My visualization from that brainspotting session went like this:

I am walking down a shady path, down into a beautiful green meadow. I am gently shedding my roles and my expectations of myself one by one as I descend into the valley where the meadow is nestled between two mountains. I see that it is ringed with aspen trees, leaves rustling in the breeze. The air is sunny and warm. It is quiet and serene. I am standing now in the meadow, and I realize I have become simply

my spirit. My pure soul. My soul which holds my spark of the Divine—
God—within me. I am free of blame and judgement of myself. I know
this because I feel lightness emanating from the crown of my head and an
absence of tightness in my shoulders. My third chakra, my solar plexus, is
shining strong and free from any judgment.

I see my other self, burdened, standing nearby. I can feel how heavy she
is with judgement. I can't tell her to let that go, to stop adding to her burden;
words don't seem to work down here in the meadow. Words have been my
help, my comfort, my way of traveling through the world. But I can't seem
to form the words I need to say to her. Ah, yes—it's because I'm pure spirit.
So, I reach for her hand and hold it. Now I am holding the hand of my
burdened self. I send lightness and love and acceptance into her hand from
mine, and I can feel it coursing through me, too, because we are joined as
one woman. We walk together, holding hands, pausing when we feel like it.

After a while, I am ready to leave the meadow. I walk back up the
path. I don't ignore the roles on the side of the path I had shed like cloth-
ing I didn't want to wear anymore. I pick them up and put them back
on, but I do not become one with them. I carry them lightly on my body,
knowing my performance in those roles does not need to define me. I can,
and I will, make mistakes in those roles, but no matter what those mis-
takes are, I am still me, not deserving of blame or judgment. At the top
of the path, I look back on the meadow below me, and I know that I can
travel back there whenever I need.

As my visualization of this beautiful meadow ended in Josh's
office, I was overcome with a sense of mercy toward myself. I said
to myself, "Robin, you truly did the best you could. You always do.
Let that be enough."

I remembered in my research on horses as power animals that
they can carry only so many burdens before they get weary and
need to lighten their load. They may collapse, and simply refuse to
go any further. I was not going to let that happen to me ever again.

I had been carrying the burden of multiple losses since Ethan died. It is very difficult to grieve multiple losses that come at you one right after the other. My body, heart, and soul at one point simply broke from grief. I stopped. I was stilled. I had developed a trauma disorder that has been thankfully responding almost miraculously to brainspotting. I had to lighten my load, a load made heavier due to my own judgement of myself. I was helped slowly back up with the support of compassionate healers. The resiliency that I was building with their help held me in good stead as more loss came our way.

Two days after we agreed to design our own separation, Jeff was diagnosed with Parkinson's disease. We were stunned. Mercy was what God guided me to show my husband. I invited him home for dinner that day of the diagnosis. No one should be alone after that kind of news. The impact of this type of disease to Jeff's short-term and long-term health was scary and daunting. We left the appointment with the neurologist and each drove back to our home in separate cars. Together we made the decision that he would remain at home. The work God led me to do on radical forgiveness, living with uncertainty, having patience, and trusting His loving hand holding mine, steadies me as my husband and I figure out how to navigate this new challenge together.

Jeff and I are currently working on building a new relationship. I don't know for certain what the future looks like for us as life partners. He is doing much healing work himself now. I'm not sure yet if we can heal our wounds as a couple. We will see. I can only be my best loving self and walk on this new path with Jeff one day at a time, one step at a time.

Chapter 32

ME AND MY TRIBE ON THE YELLOW BRICK ROAD

In my brainspotting work with Josh, he encouraged me to develop what is called a "resource" that I can access when I feel overwhelmed by grief, loss, panic, or fear of being abandoned, left alone. He had me focus on how I feel in my body when those feelings are activated and take over, and then look inside myself for a resource that I have to rely upon. Developing a resource is a key tenet of brainspotting. This resource is most helpful when it is experienced viscerally in the body, not cognitively in the mind. What spontaneously came to me as I found a gaze-spot to look at was this: a beautiful image of a shining clear path of well-placed bricks, each lit from within with a soft golden light. It looks like the yellow brick road from *The Wizard of Oz*. The path is never dark, or hard to see, because of this steady golden light. This path stretches back one direction into the past, beyond when I was born, and it stretches the other direction into the future far beyond when I leave my physical body behind on this Earth and I am in Heaven.

On this path I am never alone. Walking with me are sisters—my soul sisters—JeMae, who I believe was my sister in a former life; Jenny, who literally has walked with me many, many miles; I see

Leslie and Mary stepping onto the path, the three of us connected through threads that brought us together in ways only God could orchestrate; Becky, who loved my son as her own, and me too, even when I was at my worst; I see JoEllyn on the path, who was my professional mentor and came back into my life twenty years later; Lynn, Colette, and Kathy who have known me for thirty years and still love me; Radhe, Linda, and Sally who are my living, breathing, self-help manual; and other women, such as Tanya, who have stepped onto the path with me as new friends.

I am safe on this path, secure in my next steps, holding on to the hands of my soul sisters, even when I am not sure what the next bend in the path holds for me. God has blessed me beyond what I expected. Yet, it is what I deserve, what we all deserve. A tribe with whom to journey through black seas, red fire, grey confusion, to golden sunrises and sparkling hope.

Chapter 33
SPIRIT SON

"This life is only the cover and the title page:
now at last begins Chapter One of the Great Story,
which no one on Earth has read; which goes on forever;
in which every chapter is better than the one before."
– C.S. Lewis

Toward the end of putting my journey into words, I had reached a particularly difficult place in writing my story. Living this journey has required me to take many hard steps. I am learning how to have a relationship with my spirit son. This journey has tested me to confront truths about myself that were humbling to face. It has led me to learn what my soul's sacred contract is and to how to develop a plan to stay true to that contract. It has challenged me to let go of entrenched ways of treating myself that were no longer serving me. My suffering has prompted changes necessary for my spiritual growth. It returned me to God. Sitting down in front of my computer to write was at times an unexpected joy, but most often it was so very, very hard. Writing required me to relive the wrenching pain of this journey. But, it also gifted me with the opportunity to glean more understanding from it. The better I can communicate what I have learned, the more likely it is that sharing my story might help another person grieving their own loss.

One morning, I had told myself I would be seated in front of my computer writing by 9:00 a.m. sharp. Anyone who knows me knows that "sharp" is a fluid term even when I'm at my best. I have tried to keep a rhythm of a work week, Monday through Friday, since I left my job. But that day, I found a task, then a second task to do, then another—each one taking me blessedly further from the difficult chapter I planned to write that day. There was no way to skip over it; it had to be faced and written. Yet, by 11:00 a.m. I was in major procrastination mode. I had decided the concrete floor in the basement laundry room needed vacuuming and then scrubbing on my hands and knees. I was going to eradicate whatever was attracting all of those awful centipedes. I turned the overhead light on, and the lightbulb blew out. As I was preparing to dive into this most effective procrastination project of replacing the bulb so I could see better to wash the floor, my pup Roxy, who follows me everywhere in my house, suddenly stood stock-still in the laundry room. She cocked her head at attention. She ran into the dark storage room, stood at attention again, listening hard and quivering. She ran back through the laundry room, into the rec room, and sat still. She whined softly and wagged her tail, looking intently straight ahead.

At that very moment, a thought flashed into my head. I recalled a conversation I once had with Ethan over the phone when he was telling me he was procrastinating going to a Narcotics Anonymous meeting. I said to him, "Ethan, you have to step into the tough thing. Do it, face it, walk toward it. Don't avoid the thing that will help you because it seems to be hard." I heard my voice preaching to him and then I knew. He was right here. His spirit was here; Roxy could sense it. I know that spirits communicate through our dreams, in symbols, and through our thoughts. They can also manipulate electricity, because they are pure energy. Ethan put himself into my thoughts and got my attention, just when I needed him most. It was as if I heard

him say, "Go upstairs and do the tough thing, Mom, it will help you. Dive into it, even though it is hard. You can do it!"

Our lives here on this Earth are just the beginning of our stories, or one of many beginnings. Ethan's story was not finished when he died. And my story is not near being finished either. I sense that I will be here on Earth, in my physical body, a long time. While here on Earth, it seems so long until I am with Ethan again. In contrast, waiting to be rejoined with his family in Heaven must seem like only a blink of an eye to Ethan. Spirits experience time much differently than we do since they exist in eternity. So, I will wait, focusing on my soul's work I am to do here. Ethan's destiny, on the other hand, seems to be to accomplish much of his soul's growth in Heaven. I have come to accept that this may be the way Ethan's sacred contract is to unfold. Until I am in Heaven, I treasure the signs I receive from my spirit son, letting me know he is near. I have worked hard to free my relationship with Ethan from the pain and sorrow that had complicated it when he was so ill in his physical body. The fading pain allows love to shine more brightly between us.

I want to share with you, reader, that someone *can* thrive after such a devastating loss. I am doing more than surviving the trauma of losing my son; I have grown from this loss. This is called post-traumatic growth. When the grief overtakes me, it is rarely a dark roiling sea of pain. I rock with the waves of missing Ethan as they flow through me, knowing the waves will be calm again. Now, I am more often moving and living in a calmer sea of equanimity, even sometimes tranquility. I am deeply grateful for the healers who have helped me to be in such a place.

Perhaps Ethan and I are indeed accompanying each other, as the shaman told me. Maybe we are accompanying each other through many lifetimes, moving through time here on Earth, and then back into the afterlife. Helping each other learn the lessons we are meant to learn. If that is true, I am glad to be traveling with you, Ethan.

I am also blessed to be traveling with my tribe here. I am not alone. If I listen well, and do what God is leading me to do, I will fulfill my sacred contract, and I will make the time I have left here meaningful. I am healthier. I am better able to help others heal and grow. I am trying to reflect back to others the love and the light that I know is within me.

I am blessed to watch my other child, my daughter, be a gift to this world every day. I knew I wanted to give her the name "Deva" before I even knew what the word meant. It is a Sanskrit word that means "spirit-filled." How rich am I to have my spirit-filled daughter here on earth and my spirit son in Heaven! I will try to learn the remaining lessons of my sacred contract before I leave my physical body and join Ethan, my grandmother, and my other guides in the spirit world. I will hold the hands of my Creator and my tribe as I walk forward on that golden brick path into the destiny that I have the privilege to share with my son Ethan.

Acknowledgements

I am thankful to all of my soul sisters for walking with me on this journey. I am grateful to JeMae Guertin for repeatedly encouraging me to be brave and share my story. I am grateful to Kate Nesheim, whose sensitively delivered feedback helped me to tell my story in the most honest and clear way I possibly could. My brother Rolf was a bit less sensitive in his feedback, but equally on point. I am grateful to all of the behavioral health providers who treated my son over the almost nine years he suffered from depression and addiction. You work in one of the most challenging fields there is and you gave my son kindness, compassion, and your best effort. Thank you, dear Ariana, for loving Ethan. I am grateful for my daughter Deva who is one of the wisest and strongest young women I know. I love you so very much. I am thankful for my husband Jeff. We parented and loved Ethan during his battle with opioid addiction to the very best of our ability. We gave him our all. It is now our time to give to ourselves and each other.

Discussion Questions

1. There are many healing interventions the author seeks out and experiences in her grief journey. What interventions worked for the author and which ones did not? Why?
2. Is it possible for a healer to heal oneself, or does a healing professional need to rely on others?
3. How does she reconcile her Christian faith with her non-traditional or alternative healing experiences?
4. There is a theme of forgiveness in the author's story. How does forgiveness play a role in the author's relationship with...
   - ...her son?
   - ...her husband?
   - ...her friends?
   - ...God?
   - ...herself?
5. The author and her family struggle in their relationship with Ethan, as do many families who have a loved one with the disease of addiction. If you were a parent of a young adult child with addiction, would you have supported your child differently? How so?
6. What were Ethan's efforts in his recovery journey? Were you surprised at the number of his treatment episodes and his difficulty at sustaining treatment?

7. The author vividly describes the impact of having her son die from addiction despite so many years of her effort, her husband's effort, and the effort of many treating professionals who help Ethan.
  - Does the level of trauma she suffers from surprise you?
  - What prevented the author from seeing the effects on herself of her worsening trauma sooner?
  - How does her story compare with your own knowledge or experience of a family with a child with an addiction?
8. What does the author learn about how to have a relationship with her son Ethan's spirit?
  - Do you know of anyone with a similar relationship?
  - What do you think about such a relationship?
  - Could you see yourself having such a relationship?
9. What changes does the author make in her life as a result of her son's death?
  - How do these changes enable her to enter into a relationship with her spirit son?
  - What other changes might you make if you were in her situation?
10. What can you take away from the author's efforts to cope with her loss that might help you cope with your own?

Books That Helped Me
On My Journey

Anatomy of the Spirit: The Seven Stages of Power and Healing
by Caroline Myss
(Three River Press, 1996)

Brainspotting: The Revolutionary New Therapy
for Rapid and Effective Change
by David Grand
(Sounds True, 2013)

Comfortable with Uncertainty: 108 Teachings on
Cultivating Fearlessness and Compassion
by Pema Chödrön
(Shambhala, 2003)

Communicating with the Dead: Reaching Friends and
Loved Ones Who Have Passed On to Another Dimension of Life
by Linda Georgian
(Atria Books, 1995)

Dreamland: The True Tale of America's Opiate Epidemic
by Sam Quinones
(Bloomsbury Press, 2015)

Ninety Days: A Memoir of Recovery
by Bill Clegg
(Little, Brown and Company, 2012)

Option B: Facing Adversity, Building Resilience, and Finding Joy
by Sheryl Sandberg and Adam Grant
(WH Allen, 2017)

Portrait of an Addict as a Young Man: A Memoir
by Bill Clegg
(Little, Brown and Company, 2010)

Proof of Heaven: A Neurosurgeon's Journey into the Afterlife
by Eben Alexander
(Simon & Schuster, 2012)

*Radical Forgiveness: A Revolutionary Five-Stage Process
to Heal Relationships, Let Go of Anger and Blame,
and Find Peace in Any Situation*
by Colin Tipping
(Sounds True, 2010)

Sacred Contracts: Awakening Your Divine Potential
by Caroline Myss
(Harmony, 2003)

Surviving the Loss of a Child: Support for Grieving Parents
by Elizabeth B. Brown
(Fleming H. Revell Company, 2010)

*The Eleven Questions: Everything You Ever Wanted
To Know About Life, Death, and Afterlife*
by Mark Pitstick
(Waterfront Press, 2015)

The Light Between Us: Stories From Heaven, Lessons for the Living
by Laura Lynne Jackson
(Spiegel & Grau, 2015)

*Unbroken Brain: A Revolutionary New Way
of Understanding Addiction*
by Maia Szalavitz
(St. Martin's Press, 2016)

We Don't Die: George Anderson's Conversations with The Other Side
by Joel Martin and Patricia Romanowski
(Berkley, 1989)

When the Heart Waits: Spiritual Direction for Life's Sacred Questions
by Sue Monk Kidd
(HarperOne, 2016)

*Yoga for Grief and Loss: Poses, Meditation, Devotion,
Self-Reflection, Selfless Acts, Ritual*
by Karla Helbert
(Singing Dragon, 2015)

NATIONAL**HELPLINE**

Substance Abuse and Mental Health Services Administration's (SAMHSA) National Helpline – 1-800-662-HELP (4357)

SAMHSA's National Helpline is a free, confidential, 24/7, 365-day-a-year treatment referral and information service (in English and Spanish) for individuals and families facing mental and/or substance use disorders.

Major depression is one of the most common mental health disorders in the world, so it's likely someone you know or love has been affected. Knowing how to talk to someone living with depression can be a great way to support them.

While reaching out to someone with depression can't cure them, social support can remind them they're not alone. This can be hard to believe when depressed, but can also be incredibly helpful in a crisis.

If you or someone you know is contemplating suicide, help is out there. Reach out to the National Suicide Prevention Hotline at 800-273-8255 for free, confidential support 24/7.